Hot 'n Spicy

BY

THE EDITORS OF TIME-LIFE BOOKS

TIME-LIFE/GEDDES & GROSSET

Contents

Hot 'n Spicy

HOME COOKING

© 1994 Time-Life Books B.V.
First published jointly by Time-Life Books B.V. and
Geddes & Grosset Ltd.

Material in this book was first published as part of the
series HEALTHY HOME COOKING.

ISBN 0 7054 2044 2

Printed in Italy.

Hot 'n Spicy

Included in this volume of hot and spicy recipes are dishes inspired by ethnic cuisines from around the world. Both traditional and modern preparations and cooking techniques are imaginatively employed to make the most of the wonderful variety of foodstuffs available to the adventurous cook today.

By mixing a broad variety of main dishes with an exciting range of vegetable accompaniments, it is intended that this selection of recipes should appeal to all tastes and appetites. As always in the *Home Cooking* series there is an emphasis on good, nutritional meals which can meaningfully contribute to a balanced and healthy diet.

The Key to Better Eating

Home Cooking addresses the concerns of today's weight-conscious, health-minded cooks with recipes that take into account guidelines set by nutritionists. The secret of eating well, of course, has to do with maintaining a balance of foods in the diet. The recipes thus should be used thoughtfully, in the context of a day's eating. To make the choice easier, an analysis is given of nutrients in a single serving. The counts for calories, protein, cholesterol, total fat, saturated fat and sodium are approximate.

Interpreting the chart

The chart below gives dietary guidelines for healthy men, women and children. Recommended figures vary from country to country, but the principles are the same everywhere. Here, the average daily amounts of calories and protein are from a report by the UK Department of Health and Social Security; the maximum advisable daily intake of fat is based on guidelines given by the National Advisory Committee on Nutrition Education (NACNE); those for cholesterol and sodium are based on upper limits suggested by the World Health Organization.

The volumes in the Home Cooking series do not purport to be diet books, nor do they focus on health foods. Rather, they express a common-sense approach to cooking that uses salt, sugar, cream, butter and oil in moderation while employing other ingredients that also provide flavour and satisfaction. The portions themselves are modest in size.

The recipes make few unusual demands. Naturally they call for fresh ingredients, offering substitutes when these are unavailable. (The substitute is not calculated in the nutrient analysis, however.)

Most of the ingredients can be found in any well-stocked supermarket.

Heavy-bottomed pots and pans are recommended to guard against burning whenever a small amount of oil is used and where there is danger of the food adhering to the hot surface, but non-stick pans can be utilized as well. Both safflower oil and virgin olive oil are favoured for sautéing. Safflower oil was chosen because it is the most highly polyunsaturated vegetable fat available in supermarkets, and polyunsaturated fats reduce blood cholesterol; if unobtainable, use sunflower oil, also high in polyunsaturated fats. Virgin olive oil is used because it has a fine fruity flavour lacking in the lesser grade known as "pure". In addition, it is—like all olive oil—high in mono-unsaturated fats, which are thought not to increase blood cholesterol. When virgin olive oil is unavailable, or when its flavour is not essential to the success of the dish, 'pure' may be used.

About cooking times

To help planning, time is taken into account in the recipes. While recognizing that everyone cooks at a different speed and that stoves and ovens differ, approximate "working" and "total" times are provided. Working time stands for the minutes actively spent on preparation; total time includes unattended cooking time, as well as time devoted to marinating, steeping or soaking ingredients. Since the recipes emphasize fresh foods, they may take a bit longer to prepare than 'quick and easy' dishes that call for canned or packaged products, but the difference in flavour, and often in nutrition, should compensate for the little extra time involved.

Recommended Dietary Guidelines

Average Daily Intake			Maximum Daily Intake			
	Calories	Protein grams	Cholesterol milligrams	Total fat grams	Saturated fat grams	Sodium milligrams
Females 7-8	1900	47	300	80	32	2000*
9-11	2050	51	300	77	35	2000
12-17	2150	53	300	81	36	2000
18-54	2150	54	300	81	36	2000
55-74	1900	47	300	72	32	2000
Males 7-8	1980	49	300	80	33	2000
9-11	2280	57	300	77	38	2000
12-14	2640	66	300	99	44	2000
15-17	2880	72	300	108	48	2000
18-34	2900	72	300	109	48	2000
35-64	2750	69	300	104	35	2000
65-74	2400	60	300	91	40	2000

* (or 5g salt)

Spicy Sweetcorn Sticks

Makes about 18 sticks or wedges
Working time: about 15 minutes
Total time: about 30 minutes
Per stick: Calories 95, Protein 3g, Cholesterol 15mg, Total
fat 2g, Saturated fat 0g, Sodium 85mg

175 g/6 oz *plain flour*
125 g/4 oz *cornmeal*
2 tbsp *caster sugar*
¼ tsp *cayenne pepper*
1 tbsp *baking powder*
¼ litre/8 fl oz *semi-skimmed milk*
1 *egg*
2 tbsp *safflower oil*
6 tbsp *diced sweet red pepper*
6 tbsp *diced sweet green pepper*
90 g/3 oz *fresh or frozen sweetcorn kernels*

Preheat oven to 230°C (450°F or Mark 8). Lightly oil a corn-stick tin or a 25 cm (10 inch) stainless steel pie plate; heat in the oven for 10 minutes.

Meanwhile, put the flour, cornmeal, sugar, cayenne pepper and baking powder into a bowl and mix them together. In another bowl, whisk together the milk, egg and oil. Pour the milk mixture into the dry ingredients and stir them just until they are blended. Stir in the red and green peppers and the sweetcorn.

If using a corn-stick tin, spoon the batter into the hot tin, filling each mould about three-quarters full. Reduce the oven temperature to 200°C (400°F or Mark 6) and bake the sticks until a wooden toothpick inserted into the centre comes out clean—10 to 12 minutes. Keep the sticks warm while you bake the remaining batter. Five minutes before the last sweetcorn sticks have finished baking, return the other sticks to the oven to reheat them. Serve at once.

If using a pie plate, spoon the batter into the plate, reduce the heat to 200°C (400°F or Mark 6) and bake for about 25 minutes; cut into wedges to serve.

Aromatic Leg of Lamb

TURNING THE LAMB AND BASTING IT AT REGULAR INTERVALS DURING
COOKING KEEPS THE JUICES WITHIN THE MEAT AND ENSURES A
SUCCULENT JOINT.

Serves 12
Working time: about 1 hour
Total time: about 27 hours (includes marinating)
Calories 250, Protein 21g, Cholesterol 80mg, Total fat
12g, Saturated fat 5g, Sodium 170mg

15 cl/¹/₄ pint	plain low fat yoghurt
1 tbsp	fresh lemon juice
1 tbsp	ground coriander
2 tsp	ground cinnamon
1 tsp	ground cardamom
1 tsp	ground ginger
¹/₂ tsp	ground cloves
	freshly ground black pepper
1 tbsp	virgin olive oil
2.5 kg/5 lb	leg of lamb, boned, trimmed of fat and opened out flat
¹/₂ tsp	salt
1 tbsp	black poppy seeds
1 tbsp	white sesame seeds
1	pitta-style flat bread (optional)
	Citrus-yoghurt sauce
400 g/14 oz	thick Greek yoghurt
1	lemon, finely grated rind only
2 tbsp	fresh lemon balm, finely chopped

In a small bowl, stir together the low-fat yoghurt,
lemon juice, coriander, cinnamon, cardamom, ginger,
cloves and some black pepper to form a light paste.
Spread the paste all over the lamb. Place the lamb in a
large, flat dish, cover it and leave the meat to marinate in the refrigerator for at least 24 hours, or up to
three days. Remove the meat from the refrigerator at
least 2 hours before you plan to cook it.

Lay the meat out to form a rough rectangle. Thread
two metal skewers through the meat, each about 7.5
cm (3 inches) from the edge of a long side; this will
keep the meat flat while it is cooking. Set the barbe-
cue rack at its lowest position and brush it lightly with
oil. Sear each side of the joint over hot coals for 5 to 8
minutes, or until the surface is caramelized and lightly
charred. Remove the meat from the rack and adjust
the rack to its highest position. Return the meat to
the rack. Brush one side with a little oil, sprinkle on a
little of the salt and half of the poppy seeds and
sesame seeds, and cook the lamb for a further 3 minutes. Turn the meat over, brush it with oil, sprinkle on
the remaining salt, poppy seeds and sesame seeds,
and grill the meat for 3 minutes. Turn the joint four
more times, brushing it each time with any remaining
marinade or with a little oil, and grilling it for a further
3 minutes after each turn. The meat should be crisp
and dark on the outside, but still tender and pink inside. For more well-done meat, cook it for a further 4
to 6 minutes turning it once and brushing on more oil
as necessary to prevent it drying out. If you like, place
the cooked joint on a round of flat bread set on a carving surface: the bread will catch the meat juices and
may be served in chunks with the meat. Remove the
skewers, cover the meat lightly with foil and allow it
to rest for 5 to 10 minutes before carving.

Meanwhile, make the yoghurt sauce. Set 1 teaspoon of the lemon rind aside, and stir the remainder
into the yoghurt, together with the chopped lemon
balm. Sprinkle the reserved lemon rind over the yoghurt. Serve the meat accompanied by the sauce.

*EDITOR'S NOTE: Throwing cinnamon sticks and bay
leaves on to the coals for the last 5 to 10 minutes of bar-
becuing will enhance the flavour of the meat.*

Felafel with Red Pepper Relish

Serves 6

Working time: about 40 minutes

Total time: about 2 hours and 50 minutes
(includes soaking)

Calories 190, Protein 19g, Cholesterol 20mg, Total fat 7g,
Saturated fat 1g, Sodium 190mg

75 g/2½ oz	dried chick-peas, picked over
30 g/1 oz	onion, coarsely chopped
1	garlic clove, coarsely chopped
¼ tsp	ground cumin
½ tsp	garam masala
¼ tsp	chilli powder
75 g/2½ oz	fresh granary breadcrumbs
1 tbsp	chopped parsley
¼ tsp	salt
	freshly ground black pepper
1½ tbsp	beaten egg
	fig leaves, for garnish (optional)

Red pepper relish

1 tsp	safflower oil
½	sweet red pepper, seeded, deribbed and finely chopped
1	small onion, finely chopped
1	garlic clove, crushed
2 tbsp	malt vinegar
½ tsp	dry mustard
2 tsp	sugar
⅛ tsp	Tabasco sauce

Rinse the chick-peas under cold running water, then put them in a large, heavy-bottomed saucepan and pour in enough cold water to cover them by about 7.5 cm (3 inches). Discard any that float to the surface. Cover the pan, leaving the lid ajar, and slowly bring the liquid to the boil over medium-low heat. Boil the chick-peas for 2 minutes, then turn off the heat and soak them for at least 1 hour. (Alternatively, soak the peas overnight in cold water.)

Drain the peas; return them to the pan and cover them with at least twice their volume of fresh water. Bring the liquid to the boil, reduce the heat to maintain a strong simmer, and cook the peas until they are tender—about 1 hour.

Drain the peas and put them in a food processor with the onion and garlic. Process for about 1 minute, until the mixture is smooth. Turn the mixture into a bowl and add the cumin, garam masala and chili powder, 45 g (1½ oz) of the breadcrumbs, the parsley, salt, some pepper and ½ tablespoon of the beaten egg. Mix all the ingredients together thoroughly.

Preheat the oven to 190°C (375°F or Mark 5). Clean the food processor, and lightly oil a non-stick baking pan. Gather the chick-pea mixture into a ball and,

working on a damp board, shape it into a long roll. Cut the roll into six equal portions, then use a metal spatula to form each portion into a diamond shape on the board. Slide the spatula under one of the diamonds, lift it off the board, brush the top and sides with beaten egg and cover them with breadcrumbs, pressing the crumbs on gently. Turn the diamond over and coat the second side with beaten egg and breadcrumbs. Coat the remaining diamonds in the same way, and place all six in the baking pan.

Bake the felafel for 15 minutes, then turn them over and bake them for a further 15 minutes. Leave them to cool. Cover the felafel and chill them until required.

For the relish, heat the oil in a small, heavy frying pan and cook the red pepper, onion and garlic over low heat for 1 minute. Add the remaining ingredients, and 5 tablespoons of water, then cover the pan and simmer the mixture gently for 10 minutes. Remove the lid and simmer for a further 5 minutes, then pour the contents into the cleaned food processor and process briefly, until the ingredients are just combined. Allow the relish to cool, then chill it until required.

To serve, spread the fig leaves on a serving plate and place the felafel on top. Transfer the relish to a serving bowl.

Mexican Beef Brochettes

Serves 4

Working time: about 25 minutes

Total time: about 5 hours (includes marinating)

Calories 250, Protein 27g, Cholesterol 55mg, Total fat
15g, Saturated fat 4g, Sodium 155mg

---

500 g/1 lb *rump steak, in one or two slices about 1
cm (¹/₂ inch) thick, trimmed of fat*
2 *bay leaves*
dried bamboo leaves, for garnish (optional)
¹/₄ tsp *salt*
lime wedges, for garnish
Coriander marinade
30 g/1 oz *finely chopped onion*
1 *garlic clove, crushed*
1 to 2 *red chilli peppers, seeded and finely
chopped*
¹/₂ tsp *ground cumin*
¹/₂ tbsp *chopped fresh oregano, or ¹/₂ tsp dried
oregano*
¹/₂ tsp *paprika*
¹/₂ tsp *ground cinnamon*

6 *cloves*
1 tbsp *sesame seeds*
2 tbsp *finely chopped fresh coriander*
1¹/₂ tbsp *safflower oil*
1 tbsp *fresh lime juice*

In a shallow dish, combine all the ingredients for the
marinade. Cut the rump steak into strips about 15 cm
(6 inches) long and 6 mm (¹/₄ inch) wide, and stir them
into the marinade together with the bay leaves. Cover
the dish and put the meat in the refrigerator to marinate for at least 4 hours, or overnight, turning it once
or twice during this time. Remove the beef from the
refrigerator at least 30 minutes before cooking.

Soak eight wooden skewers in water for 10 minutes. Thread the meat strips on to the skewers, sprinkling on any remaining marinade. Cook the brochettes over hot coals for 5 to 8 minutes, turning
them frequently.

Transfer the brochettes to a serving plate lined with
dried bamboo leaves, if you are using them. Sprinkle
the brochettes with the salt and serve them garnished with the lime wedges.

Couscous Soup with Harissa

HARISSA IS A HOT, SPICY MIXTURE USED TO FLAVOUR NORTH AFRICAN DISHES; IN THIS RECIPE, SOME PIMIENTOS ARE ADDED.

Serves 8
Working time about 40 minutes
Total time: about 1 hour and 15 minutes
Calories 360, Protein 25g, Cholesterol 50mg, Total fat
15g, Saturated fat 4g, Sodium 750mg

1 tbsp	olive oil
15 g/¹/₂ oz	unsalted butter
1	large onion, coarsely chopped
¹/₂ tsp	cayenne pepper
¹/₂ tsp	ground cumin
¹/₂ tsp	cumin seeds
1 tsp	salt
¹/₂ tsp	cracked black peppercorns
¹/₂ tsp	ground allspice
4 tsp	chopped fresh thyme, or 1 tsp dried thyme
2 tsp	chopped fresh oregano, or ¹/₂ tsp dried oregano
2	bay leaves
2 or 3	garlic cloves, finely chopped (about 1 tbsp)
1.25 kg/2¹/₂ lb	ripe tomatoes, skinned, seeded and chopped, or 800 g (28 oz) canned tomatoes, drained and chopped
2 litres/3¹/₂ pints	unsalted chicken stock
1	large waxy potato, peeled and cut into 1 cm (¹/₂ inch) cubes
5	sticks celery, cut into 1 cm (¹/₂ inch) lengths
3	carrots, sliced into 5 mm (¹/₄ inch) thick rounds
500 g/1 lb	boneless chicken breast meat, cut into 2.5 cm (1 inch) cubes
125 g/4 oz	chorizo or other spicy sausage, cut into 1 cm (¹/₂ inch) thick rounds
350 g/12 oz	cooked and drained chick-peas
2	courgettes, preferably 1 green and 1 yellow, each cut lengthwise into 8 strips, the strips cut into 2.5 cm (1 inch) pieces
¹/₂	sweet green pepper, seeded, deribbed and cut lengthwise into 5 mm (¹/₄ inch) strips
¹/₂	sweet red pepper, seeded, deribbed and cut lengthwise into 5 mm (¹/₄ inch) strips
45 g/1¹/₂ oz	couscous

Harissa

175 g/6 oz	pimientos, drained
1	garlic clove
1 tsp	Tabasco sauce
2 tsp	chilli paste
2 tsp	ground cumin
¹/₄ tsp	salt

Heat the oil and butter in a large, heavy-bottomed saucepan over medium-high heat. Add the onion and sauté it, stirring frequently, until it is translucent—about 8 minutes. Meanwhile, combine the spices with the thyme, oregano and bay leaves in a small bowl.

Add the garlic to the onions and cook the mixture, stirring constantly, for 2 minutes more. Add the combined spices and herbs, tomatoes and stock, then increase the heat, and bring the liquid to the boil. Stir in the potato, celery and carrots. Reduce the heat, cover the pan, and simmer the mixture until the potato cubes are tender—about 20 minutes.

Add the chicken, sausage, chick-peas, courgettes, peppers and couscous, and simmer for 20 minutes.

While the soup finishes cooking, purée the harissa ingredients in a food processor or blender. Transfer the mixture to a small bowl. Serve the soup hot; allow each diner to add a dab of harissa if desired.

Fish Soup
with Red Pepper Sauce

Serves 6

Working (and total) time: about 45 minutes

Calories 205, Protein 17g, Cholesterol 35mg, Total fat 9g,
Saturated fat 1g, Sodium 160mg

1.5 litres/2½ pints	*fish stock*
3	*large leeks, green tops discarded, white parts split, washed thoroughly to remove all grit, and thinly sliced*
250 g/8 oz	*finely shredded Savoy cabbage*
2	*ripe tomatoes, skinned, seeded and chopped*
500 g/1 lb	*fillet from a firm, white-fleshed fish such as cod, rinsed and cut into 2.5 cm (1 inch) chunks*
4 tbsp	*freshly grated pecorino cheese*
	Red pepper sauce
2	*wholemeal bread slices, crusts removed*
1	*sweet red pepper, seeded, deribbed and chopped*
2	*large garlic cloves, chopped*
⅛ tsp	*cayenne pepper*
3 tbsp	*virgin olive oil*

To prepare the red pepper sauce, first put the bread slices into a bowl and pour in enough water to cover them. Soak the slices for 10 minutes, then squeeze out the water and transfer the bread to a food processor. Add the red pepper, garlic and cayenne pepper, and purée the mixture. With the machine still running, dribble in the olive oil; the resulting sauce should be thick. Set the sauce aside.

For the soup, pour the stock into a large pan and bring it to the boil. Add the leeks, cabbage and tomatoes, then reduce the heat and simmer the vegetables until they are tender—about 10 minutes. Add the fish and cook the soup until the fish is firm and opaque—about 3 minutes. Pass the cheese and the red pepper sauce in separate bowls.

Plaice Curry

Serves 4

Working time: about 30 minutes

Total time: about 40 minutes

Calories 280, Protein 25g, Cholesterol 55mg, Total fat 7g,
Saturated fat 1g, Sodium 205mg

1 tbsp	*chopped fresh ginger root*
1/2 tsp	*turmeric*
1/4 tsp	*ground cumin*
1/4 tsp	*ground coriander*
1/8 tsp	*ground cardamom*
1/8 tsp	*fennel seeds*
1/8 tsp	*ground mace*
1 tbsp	*safflower oil*
2	*onions, sliced*
750 g/1 1/2 lb	*ripe tomatoes, skinned, seeded and chopped, or 400 g (14 oz) canned tomatoes, drained and crushed*
1/2 litre/16 fl oz	*fish stock or unsalted chicken stock*
500 g/1 lb	*mushrooms, wiped clean and halved*
1/2	*lemon, juice only*
500 g/1 lb	*plaice fillets (or other white-fleshed fish)*

Put the ginger, turmeric, cumin, coriander, cardamom, fennel seeds and mace into a mortar; with a pestle, grind the seasonings to a paste. Set the paste aside.

Heat the oil in a large, non-reactive, heavy sauté pan over medium-high heat. Add the onions and sauté them until they are translucent—about 4 minutes. Stir in the spice paste, tomatoes and stock, and bring the liquid to the boil. Add the mushrooms and lemon juice. Lower the heat and simmer the curry until it is reduced by half—8 to 12 minutes.

Meanwhile, rinse the fillets under cold running water and pat them dry with paper towels. Slice the fillets into 2.5 cm (1 inch) wide strips. Lay the strips on top of the curry, cover the pan, and steam the fish until it is opaque—about 2 minutes. Serve immediately.

Java Lamb Curry with Tamarind

Serves 4
Working time: about 30 minutes
Total time: about 1 hour and 30 minutes

Calories 375, Protein 24g, Cholesterol 55mg,   Total fat 24g, Saturated fat 13g, Sodium 380mg

500 g/1 lb	lean, boneless lamb (preferably leg or shoulder), cut into 2.5 cm (1 inch) cubes
1 tbsp	ground coriander
2 tsp	ground cumin
1/4 tsp	crushed hot red pepper flakes or chilli paste
1/2 tsp	freshly ground black pepper
1 tbsp	flour
1 tbsp	safflower oil
1	large onion, chopped
1	sweet red pepper, seeded, deribbed and chopped
1 tbsp	finely chopped fresh ginger root
2	garlic cloves, finely chopped
1/2 litre/16 fl oz	unsalted brown stock
75 g/2 1/2 oz	tamarind pulp, steeped in 12.5 cl (4 fl oz) of boiling water for 10 minutes, liquid strained and reserved
6 tbsp	unsweetened coconut milk
1/2 tsp	salt
1/8 tsp	ground cinnamon
1/8 tsp	ground cloves
1	lemon, rind julienned, juice reserved
200 g/7 oz	cauliflower florets
1	lemon (optional), sliced into thin rounds

Toss the lamb cubes with the coriander, cumin, red pepper flakes, black pepper and flour. Heat the oil in a large, heavy-bottomed pan over medium-high heat. Add the lamb cubes and sauté them, in several batches if necessary, until they are browned on all sides—about 8 minutes per batch. Stir in the onion, red pepper, ginger and garlic. Reduce the heat to medium; cover the pan and cook the mixture, stirring frequently to keep the onions from burning, for 8 minutes.

Add the stock, tamarind liquid, coconut milk, salt, cinnamon and cloves. Bring the mixture to a simmer, then reduce the heat so that the liquid barely trembles; cover the pan and cook the mixture for 45 minutes.

Stir in the lemon rind, lemon juice and cauliflower. Continue to simmer the curry, covered, until the cauliflower is tender—about 15 minutes. If you like, garnish the curry with the lemon slices before serving.

EDITOR'S NOTE: Tamarind pulp—the peeled, compressed flesh of a tropical plant native to India—is available in many markets, including those specializing in Indian and Latin American foods.

If canned or frozen unsweetened coconut milk is not available, the coconut milk may be made at home: mix 6 tablespoons of desiccated coconut in a blender with 6 tablespoons of very hot water, then strain the liquid.

Prawn Creole

Serves 4

Working time: about 35 minutes

Total time: about 1 hour and 15 minutes

Calories 325, Protein 23g, Cholesterol 165mg, Total fat 6g, Saturated fat 1g, Sodium 240mg

4 tsp	safflower oil
1	large onion, thinly sliced
2	garlic cloves, finely chopped
1 tbsp	flour
1 tbsp	chilli powder
600 g/1¼ lb	large uncooked prawns, peeled, deveined if necessary, shells reserved
¼ litre/8 fl oz	dry white vermouth
90 g/3 oz	long-grain rice
3	small sweet green peppers, seeded, deribbed and cut lengthwise into thin strips
1	stick celery, thinly sliced on the diagonal
750 g/1½ lb	ripe tomatoes, skinned, seeded and coarsely chopped, with their juice, or 400 g (14 oz) canned tomatoes, chopped, with their juice
¼ tsp	filé powder (optional)
¼ tsp	salt
30 g/1 oz	lean ham (optional), julienned

Heat 2 teaspoons of the oil in a heavy-bottomed saucepan over medium heat. Add the onion slices and cook them, stirring frequently, until they are browned—8 to 10 minutes. Remove half of the slices and set them aside.

Add the garlic and cook it for 1 minute. Stir in the flour and chilli powder, then the prawn shells, vermouth and ¼ litre (8 fl oz) of water. Bring the liquid to a simmer; reduce the heat to medium low, cover the pan and cook the mixture for 20 minutes to make a flavourful base for the stew.

Meanwhile, bring ¼ litre (8 fl oz) of water to the boil in a small saucepan. Add the rice, stir once and reduce the heat to maintain a simmer; cook the rice, covered, until the liquid is absorbed—about 20 minutes. Set the rice aside while you finish the stew.

Heat the remaining oil in a large, heavy frying pan over medium-high heat. Add the prawns to the pan and sauté them, stirring, for 2 minutes. Stir in the peppers and celery and cook them for 1 minute. Add the tomatoes, the reserved onion slices and the filé powder if you are using it. Strain the stew base into the frying pan and add the rice. Gently simmer the stew for 5 minutes. Stir in the salt and garnish the stew with the ham, if you are using it, just before serving.

EDITOR'S NOTE: Filé powder, used to flavour and thicken Creole soups and stews, is made from dried young sassafras leaves.

18

Thai Prawn Soup with Lemon Grass

Serves 6 as a first course
Working time: about 30 minutes
Total time: about 45 minutes
Calories 50, Protein 6g, Cholesterol 40mg, Total fat 0g,
Saturated fat 0g, Sodium 180mg

2 tsp	*safflower oil*
250 g/8 oz	*fresh prawns, peeled, deveined if necessary and halved lengthwise, the shells reserved*
60 cl/1 pint	*unsalted chicken stock*
2	*stalks lemon grass, the root ends and woody tops trimmed off, the stalks cut into 2.5 cm (1 inch) long pieces, or 1 tsp grated lemon rind*
4 tbsp	*fresh lime juice*
1/2 tsp	*sambal oelek or crushed hot red pepper flakes*
2 tsp	*fish sauce*
6	*paper-thin slices of lime for garnish fresh coriander leaves for garnish (optional)*

Heat the oil in a heavy pan over medium heat. Add the prawn shells and cook them, stirring, until they turn bright pink—about 1 minute. Add the stock, 60 cl (1 pint) of water and the lemon grass if you are using it. (If you are substituting lemon rind, do not add it yet.) Bring the liquid to the boil, then reduce the heat to medium low, cover the pan, and simmer the mixture for 5 minutes. Turn off the heat and let the liquid stand for 15 minutes.

Strain the stock into a bowl. Discard the solids and return the liquid to the pan. Bring the liquid to a simmer and add the lime juice, crushed red pepper flakes, fish sauce and prawns. If you are using lemon rind, add it now. Cook the soup until the prawns are opaque—about 1 minute. To serve, ladle the soup into bowls and garnish each one with a lime slice and, if you like, some coriander leaves.

EDITOR'S NOTE: Fish sauce is available in well-stocked supermarkets; fresh lemon grass and sambal oelek may be purchased in Asian grocery shops.

Seafood Chilli with Peppers

Serves 4

Working time: about 1 hour and 30 minutes

Total time: about 3 hours and 30 minutes (includes soaking)

Calories 450, Protein 34g, Cholesterol 70mg, Total fat 14g, Saturated fat 1g, Sodium 305mg

185 g/6½ oz	dried black beans, picked over
250 g/8 oz	queen scallops, rinsed
125 g/4 oz	prawns, peeled
125 g/4 oz	haddock or monkfish fillet, rinsed and cut into pieces about 5 cm (2 inches) long and 2.5 cm (1 inch) wide
1	lime, carefully peeled to remove the white pith, sliced into thin rounds
1¼ tsp	ground cumin
⅛ tsp	ground ginger
3¼ tsp	chilli powder
3 tbsp	coarsely chopped fresh coriander
2	garlic cloves, finely chopped
½	fresh hot green chilli pepper, seeded and finely chopped
3 tbsp	safflower oil
1	onion, cut into chunks
½ tsp	dried tarragon
¼ tsp	salt
¼ tsp	ground cloves
⅛ tsp	ground cinnamon
⅛ tsp	cayenne pepper
35 cl/12 fl oz	unsalted chicken stock
400 g/14 oz	canned chopped tomatoes, with juice
10	small green tomatoes, or 10 husked tomatillos, quartered
1	sweet red pepper, seeded, deribbed and cut into chunks the size of the tomato quarters
1	sweet yellow pepper, seeded, deribbed and cut into chunks the size of the tomato quarters

Rinse the beans under cold running water, then put them into a large pan and pour in enough cold water to cover them by about 7.5 cm (3 inches). Discard any beans that float to the surface. Cover, leaving the lid ajar, and bring the liquid to the boil over medium-low heat. Boil the beans for 2 minutes, then turn off the heat, cover the pan, and soak them for at least 1 hour. (Alternatively, soak the beans overnight in cold water.)

Drain the beans in a colander and return them to the pan. Pour in enough water to cover the beans by about 7.5 cm (3 inches), and bring the liquid to the boil over medium-low heat. Reduce the heat to maintain a strong simmer and cover the pan. Cook the beans, stirring occasionally and skimming any foam from the surface, until they are tender—1½ to 2 hours.

While the beans are cooking, combine in a large non-reactive bowl the scallops, prawns, fish pieces, lime, ¼ teaspoon of the cumin, the ginger, ¼ teaspoon of the chilli powder, 1 tablespoon of the fresh coriander, half of the garlic, the chilli pepper and 1 tablespoon of the oil. Marinate for 30 minutes at room temperature.

While the seafood is marinating, prepare the chilli base. Heat 1 tablespoon of the remaining oil in a large heavy-bottomed saucepan over medium heat. Add the onion and remaining garlic, and cook until the onion is translucent—about 5 minutes. Add the remaining cumin, the remaining chilli powder, the tarragon, salt, cloves, cinnamon and cayenne pepper. Cook, stirring constantly, for 2 to 3 minutes to meld the flavours.

Gradually stir in the stock and tomatoes, and bring the mixture to the boil. Reduce the heat to medium low and cover the pan, leaving the lid slightly ajar. Simmer the liquid until it is slightly thickened—20 to 25 minutes. Drain the beans and add them to the tomato mixture. Set the chilli base aside.

Pour the remaining oil into a large, heavy frying pan over high heat. Add the green tomatoes or tomatillos and the pepper chunks, and sauté for 2 minutes. Using a slotted spoon, carefully spread the cooked vegetables over the chili base; bring the mixture to a simmer over low heat. Lay the marinated seafood on top of the vegetables, cover, and steam until the scallops and fish are opaque—7 to 10 minutes. Sprinkle the remaining coriander over the chili and serve immediately.

EDITOR'S NOTE: A tomatillo is a small tart green fruit vegetable in the Physalis family. It is not widely available in Europe, but is an authentic ingredient of this dish in Mexico. Warm corn tortillas go well with this chilli.

Curried Black-Eyed Peas

Serves 6 as a side dish
Working time: about 20 minutes
Total time: about 2 hours and 30 minutes (includes
soaking and chilling)
Calories 105, Protein 5g, Cholesterol 0mg, Total fat 3g,
Saturated fat 0g, Sodium 100mg

170 g/6 oz	black-eyed peas, picked over
1/4 tsp	salt
12.5 cl/4 fl oz	unsalted chicken stock
2	bunches spring onions, trimmed and cut into 2.5 cm (1 inch) lengths
1 1/2 tbsp	fresh lemon juice
1 tbsp	red wine vinegar or white wine vinegar
1/2 tbsp	honey
1 1/4 tsp	curry powder
	freshly ground black pepper
1 tbsp	virgin olive oil
1/2	sweet red pepper, seeded, deribbed and cut into bâtonnets

Rinse the black-eyed peas under cold running water, then put them into a large saucepan, and pour in enough cold water to cover them by about 7.5 cm (3 inches). Discard any peas that float to the surface. Bring the water to the boil and cook the peas for 2 minutes. Turn off the heat, partially cover the pan, and soak the peas for at least 1 hour. (Alternatively, soak the peas overnight in cold water.)

Bring the peas to a simmer over medium-low heat and tightly cover the pan. Cook the peas, occasionally skimming any foam from the surface of the liquid, until they begin to soften—about 45 minutes. Stir in the salt and continue cooking the peas until they are quite tender—about 15 minutes more. If the peas appear to be drying out at any point, pour in more water.

While the peas are cooking, heat the stock in a large frying pan over medium heat. Add the spring onions and partially cover the pan. Cook the spring onions, stirring often, until almost all the liquid has evaporated—8 to 10 minutes. Transfer the contents of the pan to a bowl.

In a smaller bowl, combine the lemon juice, vinegar, honey, curry powder and some pepper. Whisk in the oil and set the dressing aside.

Transfer the cooked peas to a colander; rinse and drain them. Add the peas and the red pepper to the spring onions in the bowl. Pour the dressing over all and toss the salad well. Chill the salad for at least 30 minutes before serving.

Curried Chicken Salad with Raisins

Serves 6 as a main course
Working time: about 20 minutes
Total time: about 1 hour
Calories 250, Protein 20g, Cholesterol 55mg, Total fat 9g,
Saturated fat 2g, Sodium 190mg

1 tsp	*safflower oil*
6	*chicken breasts, skinned and boned (about 750 g/1^1/$_2$ lb)*
^{1}/$_4$ tsp	*salt*
75 g/2^1/$_2$ oz	*raisins*
1	*large carrot, grated*
1	*onion, grated*
1	*stick celery, chopped*
3 tbsp	*fresh lemon juice*
1 tbsp	*curry powder*
1 tbsp	*honey*
4 tbsp	*mayonnaise*
100 g/3^1/$_2$ oz	*radishes, julienned*
^{1}/$_2$ tbsp	*virgin olive oil*
1	*small cos lettuce, washed and dried*
2	*ripe tomatoes, cut into wedges*

Heat the safflower oil in a large, heavy frying pan over low heat. Sprinkle the chicken breasts with the salt and place them in the pan. Set a heavy plate on top of the chicken breasts to weight them down so that they will cook evenly. Cook the breasts on the first side for 5 minutes; turn them over, weight them down again with the plate, and cook them on the second side for 3 to 4 minutes. The meat should feel firm but springy to the touch, with no traces of pink along the edges. Transfer the breasts to a plate and allow them to cool. When the chicken is cool enough to handle, cut it into 2.5 cm (1 inch) cubes.

In a large mixing bowl, toss the chicken cubes with the raisins, grated carrot and onion, chopped celery, lemon juice, curry powder, honey and mayonnaise. Chill the salad for at least 30 minutes.

Toss the radish julienne with the olive oil in a small bowl. Mound the chicken salad on the lettuce leaves, and garnish each plate with the radish julienne and the tomato wedges. Serve immediately.

Gingered Prawns
on Black Beans

Serves 6
Working time: about 1 hour
Total time: about 9 hours
Calories 425, Protein 30g, Cholesterol 110mg, Total fat
6g, Saturated fat 1g, Sodium 345mg

600 g/1¼ lb	*large raw prawns, peeled and deveined, the shells reserved*
2.5 cm/1 inch	*piece of fresh ginger root, peeled and thinly sliced, plus 1 tbsp chopped fresh ginger root*
35 cl/12 fl oz	*dry white wine*
500 g/1 lb	*dried black beans, soaked for at least 8 hours and drained*
2	*onions, chopped*
4	*garlic cloves, 2 crushed and 2 very thinly sliced*
1	*cinnamon stick, broken into 3 or 4 pieces freshly ground black pepper*
¼ tsp	*salt*
1 tbsp	*grated lemon rind*
2 tbsp	*virgin olive oil*
½ tsp	*ground cinnamon*
1 tsp	*fresh lemon juice*
3	*spring onions, trimmed and thinly sliced*

Put the prawn shells in a large saucepan. Add the ginger slices, ¼ litre (8 fl oz) of the wine and ½ litre (16 fl oz) of water, and bring the mixture to the boil. Reduce the heat to medium and cook until the liquid is reduced by half—about 30 minutes. Strain the stock into a bowl, pressing down on the shells to extract any liquid, and set the bowl aside.

While the shells are cooking, put the drained beans in a large, heavy-bottomed saucepan along with the onions, crushed garlic cloves, the pieces of cinnamon stick and some pepper. Pour in enough water to cover the beans by about 4 cm (1½ inches) and boil the beans for 10 minutes. Skim off the foam and reduce the heat to low. Add the prawn stock, salt and lemon rind, and simmer the mixture until the beans are tender but not mushy and a thick sauce results— 1½ to 2 hours. Remove the cinnamon stick pieces and discard them.

About 5 minutes before the beans finish cooking, pour the oil into a large, heavy frying pan over medium-high heat. When the oil is hot, add the prawns and sprinkle them with some pepper. Add the chopped ginger, the thinly sliced garlic and the ground cinnamon, and sauté the prawns, stirring frequently, for 3 minutes. Pour the lemon juice and the remaining wine into the pan; continue cooking the mixture, stirring frequently, until the prawns are opaque and the liquid is reduced to a glaze—2 to 3 minutes more. Stir in the spring onions.

Pour the beans on to a serving platter and top them with the prawn mixture. Serve immediately.

Grilled Eel
in Ginger-Sherry Sauce
on Rice Fingers

Serves 4 as a first course
Working time: about 30 minutes
Total time: about 40 minutes
Calories 420, Protein 20g, Cholesterol 95mg,
Total fat 14g, Saturated fat 3g, Sodium 370mg

500 g/1 lb *eel*
1 tsp *rice vinegar*
200 g/7 oz *glutinous rice, preferably sushi rice*
1 tsp *wasabi (Japanese horseradish powder),*
mixed with enough water to form a paste
Ginger-sherry sauce
4 tbsp *dry sherry*
2 tbsp *low-sodium soy sauce or shoyu*
1 tbsp *finely chopped fresh ginger root*
1 tbsp *sugar*
1 tbsp *honey*
1/8 tsp *cayenne pepper*

In a saucepan, bring 1/2 litre (16 fl oz) of water and the vinegar to the boil. Add the rice, tightly cover the pan and reduce the heat to medium low. Cook the rice, stirring occasionally, until all the liquid has been absorbed —about 20 minutes. Set the rice aside to cool.

While the rice is cooking, fillet the eel. Place it on its belly on a cutting board. Cut the head off behind the gills and discard it. Holding a small, sharp knife parallel to the eel, cut along one side of the dorsal fin, following the contour of the backbone along the length of the eel until the fillet is freed . Repeat the process on the other side of the fin to free the second fillet. Cut away any viscera clinging to the fillets. Rinse the fillets under cold running water and cut each in half diagonally.

Pour enough water into a large pan to fill it 1 cm (1/2 inch) deep. Put a bamboo steamer basket in the water. (Alternatively, put a heatproof cup in the centre of the pan and lay a heatproof plate on top of it.) Place the eel fillets in the steamer basket or on the plate, and bring the water to the boil. Reduce the heat to low, tightly cover the pan and steam the fillets for 7 minutes.

While the fillets are steaming, make the sauce. Combine the sherry, soy sauce, ginger, sugar, honey and cayenne pepper in a small saucepan. Bring the sauce to the boil, then reduce the heat to low. Simmer the sauce until it thickens and is reduced by half 7 to 10 minutes. Preheat the grill.

Brush some of the sauce on both sides of the fillets and let them stand for 5 minutes. Brush more sauce on the fillets and grill them 7.5 cm (3 inches) below the heat source until they are crisp—2 to 4 minutes. Carefully turn the fillets over, then brush on more sauce and grill them on the second side until they are crisp—2 to 3 minutes.

While the eel is cooking, form the cooled rice into 16 cakes (the Japanese call them "fingers"); each should be about 5 cm (2 inches) long, 2 cm (3/4 inch) wide and 2 cm (3/4 inch) thick. Arrange the rice fingers on a serving platter or individual plates.

Cut the fillets diagonally into 16 pieces. Set a piece of eel on top of each rice cake; brush the eel pieces with the remaining sauce and serve them with the wasabi.

EDITOR'S NOTE: Sushi rice, a glutinous rice whose grains cohere well when cooked, is available at Japanese food shops.

Okra Stuffed with Indian Spices

CHOOSE PLUMP, UNBLEMISHED OKRA PODS FOR STUFFING

Serves 4

Working (and total) time: about 40 minutes

Calories 60, Protein 6g, Cholesterol 10mg, Total fat 2g,
Saturated fat 1g, Sodium 125mg

20	okra
1 tsp	coriander seeds
1/2 tsp	yellow mustard seeds
4	garlic cloves
1/4 tsp	turmeric
1/2 tsp	freshly ground black pepper
1 tbsp	finely cut chives plus four whole chives, about 18 cm (7 inches) long
2 1/2 tbsp	cottage cheese

Coriander-yoghurt sauce

1/2 tsp	yellow mustard seeds
6 tbsp	thick Greek yoghurt
1/2 tsp	chopped fresh coriander leaves
1/4 tsp	white pepper
1/2	garlic clove, crushed
1 tsp	fresh lemon juice

First make the sauce. Toast the mustard seeds in a dry, heavy frying pan over medium heat for a few seconds until they begin to pop, then crush them in a mortar with a pestle. In a small bowl, stir together the yoghurt, coriander leaves, crushed mustard seeds, pepper, garlic and the lemon juice. Set the sauce aside to allow its flavours to blend while you stuff the okra.

With a sharp knife, make a slit along the length of each okra pod, being careful not to split the ends of the vegetable. Using a small knife or the tips of your fingers, remove the seeds from the okra.

Toast the coriander seeds and the mustard seeds in a dry, heavy frying pan over medium heat for a few seconds until the seeds pop and begin to release their aroma. Place the seeds in a mortar with the garlic, turmeric and black pepper and, using a pestle, pound them to a paste. Stir in the finely cut chives and the cottage cheese and continue pounding the mixture until all the ingredients are well blended.

Stuff each okra pod with a little of the paste, pressing the edges of the slit together so the stuffing will not leak out as it cooks. Wipe off any paste that still clings to the outside of the vegetables. Tie five of the stuffed okra pods together in a bundle with a long piece of chive. Repeat the process to form four bundles of the vegetables. Tuck the loose ends of the chives neatly underneath the okra parcels and place them in a steamer. Steam the okra over boiling water until they are tender and bright green—about 5 minutes.

Serve the okra bundles immediately on individual plates, accompanied by the coriander-yoghurt sauce.

Seven-Spice Stew with Mussels, Squid and Prawns

Serves 6

Working (and total) time: about 1 hour

Calories 165, Protein 17g, Cholesterol 130mg, Total fat
2g, Saturated fat 0g, Sodium 265mg

750 g/1¹/₂ lb	mussels, scrubbed and debearded
250 g/8 oz	squid, cleaned and skinned
250 g/8 oz	large raw prawns, peeled and deveined if necessary
1	onion, chopped
¹/₄ litre/8 fl oz	dry white wine
2	ripe tomatoes, skinned, seeded and chopped
1	whole garlic bulb, cloves peeled and thinly sliced
¹/₄ tsp	each ground turmeric, cumin, coriander
¹/₈ tsp	each ground allspice, cloves, cardamom
¹/₈ tsp	cayenne pepper

Put the mussels in a deep pan, together with the onion and the wine. Cover the pan tightly and cook the mussels over medium-high heat until they open—about 5 minutes. Discard any mussels that remain closed. Let the mussels cool, then remove them from their shells and set them aside. Strain the mussel-cooking liquid into a bowl and let it stand for 2 to 3 minutes to allow any sand to settle out. Slowly pour most of the liquid into a large, heavy-frying pan, leaving the sand behind.

Add the tomatoes, garlic and spices to the frying pan. Bring the liquid to the boil, then reduce the heat to medium low and simmer the mixture until the garlic is tender—about 5 minutes.

Meanwhile, prepare the squid. Slit the pouches up one side and lay them flat on the work surface. Use a sharp knife to score a criss-cross pattern on the inside of each pouch. Cut the scored pouches into 4 cm (1¹/₂ inch) squares. Chop the tentacles into small pieces.

Add the squid to the liquid simmering in the frying pan. Cover the pan and cook the mixture until the squid pieces have curled up—about 1 minute. Add the prawns, cover the pan and continue cooking until the prawns are opaque—approximately 1 minute more. Finally, add the mussels and cook the stew for 1 minute to heat the mussels through. Serve at once.

EDITOR 'S NOTE: Cooked prawns can be used instead of the raw ones; add them with the mussels at the end.

Sea Bass
Galantine Orientale

Serves 12 as a first course
Working time: about 2 hours
Total time: about 7 hours (includes marinating and chilling)
Calories 150, Protein 14g, Cholesterol 80mg, Total fat 5g,
Saturated fat 1g, Sodium 160mg

1.25 kg/2^1/$_2$ lb	sea bass, boned and gutted through the back, head and tail left intact, bones and trimmings reserved
1 tbsp	low-sodium soy sauce or shoyu
1 tbsp	light sesame oil
3 tbsp	rice vinegar
5 cm/2 inch	piece fresh ginger root, peeled
1	small carrot, sliced
1	leek, white part only, slit and cleaned thoroughly to remove all grit
1	small shallot, sliced
1	garlic clove
1	parsley sprig
1	fresh tarragon sprig
4	black peppercorns
45 cl/^{3}/$_4$ pint	dry white wine
1 tsp	powdered gelatine
2 tsp	white sesame seeds, toasted
2 tsp	black sesame seeds
1	black olive, stoned and halved whole cooked prawns, for garnish (optional)

Prawn and shiitake stuffing

60 g/2 oz	round-grain rice
1 tbsp	light sesame oil
75 g/2^1/$_2$ oz	fresh shiitake mushrooms, very finely sliced
350 g/12 oz	raw giant prawns, shells removed and reserved, prawns deveined
2	garlic cloves
2.5 cm/1 inch	piece fresh ginger root, peeled
^{1}/$_4$ tsp	salt
1 tsp	arrowroot
1	egg white
150 g/5 oz	cooked giant prawns, shells removed and reserved, prawns deveined and finely diced

Rinse the fish thoroughly and pat it dry on paper towels. Pour the soy sauce, light sesame oil and 1 tablespoon of the rice vinegar into a bowl. Using a garlic press, squeeze the juice from the ginger into the bowl. Whisk these together to make a marinade. Sit the fish, belly side down, on a dish, pour the marinade inside it, and leave it to marinate for about 1 hour.

Meanwhile, prepare the stuffing. Put the rice and

17.5 cl (6 fl oz) of water in a small saucepan and bring to the boil over medium-high heat. Reduce the heat, cover the saucepan and simmer the rice until the liquid has been absorbed and the rice is tender—about 20 minutes. Set the rice aside to cool. Heat the oil in a small frying pan and gently cook the mushrooms, covered, for about 10 minutes. Remove the lid and drain off any liquid. Set the mushrooms aside to cool.

Using a food processor or a mortar and pestle, reduce the raw prawns and the cooled rice to a paste. With a garlic press, squeeze the juices of the garlic and ginger into the prawn paste. Blend the ingredients thoroughly, then beat in the salt, arrowroot and egg white to form a fluffy mass.

Fold the diced cooked prawns into the raw prawn mixture, together with the shiitake mushrooms. Add the cooked sea bass roe, if you are using any, and stir the stuffing thoroughly.

Pour off any unabsorbed marinade from the sea bass, and pack the stuffing into the fish. Wrap the fish in a 30 cm (12 inch) square of muslin and secure it with thread. Sit the fish on its belly on the rack of a fish kettle. Pour 2.5 cm (1 inch) of boiling water into the kettle, keeping the water level below the belly of the fish.

Cover the kettle and steam the fish over medium heat for 25 to 35 minutes, or until the flesh in the middle of the back is opaque. Remove the bass from the kettle and leave it to rest, again on its belly, for 5 minutes, then invert it on to its back to drain and cool. When the fish is cool enough to handle, turn it back on to its belly, unwrap it and carefully remove the skin, leaving the head intact. Leave the fish in the refrigerator to chill thoroughly for about 1 hour.

While the fish is chilling, make the stock. Put all reserved bones and trimmings, the carrot, leek, shallot, garlic clove, parsley, tarragon, peppercorns, wine and the remaining rice vinegar in a large saucepan. Add 30 cl (^{1}/$_2$ pint) of water and simmer the liquid for 20 minutes. Strain the stock through muslin, then return it to the pan and simmer until it is reduced to about 6 tablespoons. Dissolve the gelatine in the reduced stock and set it aside until it cools and begins to set—about 20 minutes.

Place the chilled fish on a serving platter. As soon as the aspic has just begun to set, brush some of it all over the fish. Place the fish in the refrigerator for 5 minutes, then garnish it with rows of white and black sesame seeds. Spoon over the remaining aspic. Set the olive halves in the fish's eye sockets. Chill the bass for at least 2 hours before serving it, garnished with whole cooked prawns, if you wish.

EDITOR'S NOTE: To bone and gut a bass through the back, slit it from head to tail on either side of the dorsal fin and work the blade of a small, flexible knife round the rib cage of the fish. Cut the backbone at the head and tail ends with kitchen scissors, leaving both the head and tail in position. Pull out and discard the backbone, gut, entrails and gills, then rinse the fish. Alternatively, you can ask your fishmonger to bone the fish for you. If you do not have a fish kettle or steamer pan of suitable size, wrap the fish in a double layer of oiled cooking foil instead of muslin. Sit the fish on a rack in a roasting pan, pour in 2.5 cm (1 inch) of boiling water, and steam it for 25 minutes. Leave the fish to cool in the foil.

Seafood Wonton with Mango and Ginger Sauce

WONTO IN CHINESE MEANS "A MOUTHFUL OF CLOUD"; IT IS
TRADITIONALLY MADE WITH A PASTA DOUGH, AND IS OFTEN DEEP FRIED
IN OIL. IN THIS LIGHTER VERSION, PHYLLO PASTRY IS USED FOR THE
CONTAINERS, AND THE WONTONS ARE BAKED IN THE OVEN INSTEAD OF
DEEP FRIED.

Serves 6

Working (and total) time: about 1 hour and 30 minutes
Calories 240, Protein 20g, Cholesterol 85mg, Total fat 9g,
Saturated fat 2g, Sodium 230mg

1 kg/2 lb	sole or haddock, skinned and filleted, covered with plastic film and chilled
2	egg whites
1/8 tsp	white pepper
1/8 tsp	cayenne pepper
2 tbsp	dry sherry
1/4 tsp	fresh lime juice
350 g/12 oz	freshprawns, shelled, diced, covered with plastic film and refrigerated
5	shallots, finely chopped
4	sheets phyllo pastry, each 30 cm (12 inches) square
2 tbsp	safflower oil
2 tbsp	shelled peas, cooked, for garnish

Mango and ginger dipping sauce

30 cl/1/2 pint	unsalted fish stock
15 g/1/2 oz	concentrated butter
1 tsp	finely grated fresh ginger root
1	ripe mango (about 375 g/13 oz), skinned, seeded and roughly chopped
1/2	lime, juice only
1/4 tsp	salt
12	fresh coriander leaves, for garnish

Place the chilled fish in a food processor with the egg whites, pepper, cayenne pepper, sherry and lime juice, and process until it forms a smooth puree. Put the puree in a bowl and stir in the prawns and shal-

lots. Cover the bowl with plastic film and chill it in the refrigerator while you prepare the phyllo pastry.

Preheat the oven to 180°C (350°F or Mark 4).

Spread out a phyllo sheet on a floured surface. Brush it lightly with a little of the oil and place a second sheet on top of it. Using a ruler and a sharp knife, cut the double layer of phyllo into 10 cm (4 inch) squares. Repeat the process with the remaining phyllo sheets to form 18 squares.

Rub a little oil on a baking sheet. Brush both sides of the sandwiched pastry squares lightly with the remaining oil. Remove the filling from the refrigerator and put a tablespoon of seafood mixture in the centre of a square, gather up the corners and pinch them gently round the filling to form a parcel. With the aid of a sharp knife, separate the tips of the pastry corners and pull them apart to form petals. Prepare the remaining wontons in the same way and transfer them to the oiled baking sheet.

Place the baking sheet on the middle rack of the oven and bake the wontons until they are goldenbrown—15 to 20 minutes. Check them after the first 10 minutes of baking: if their tips are browning too quickly, cover the wontons with a sheet of foil.

Meanwhile, prepare the sauce. In a saucepan, boil the fish stock over high heat until it is reduced by half. In a second saucepan, melt the butter and fry the ginger until it is slightly golden. Add the chopped mango, stir until the fruit is soft—about 2 minutes—then add the reduced stock and simmer the mixture for 5 minutes. Purée the sauce in a blender, returning it afterwards to the pan to keep warm. Add the lime juice and salt.

Just before serving, place a few of the peas in the centre of each wonton and garnish the sauce with coriander leaves.

EDITOR'S NOTE: The fish bones and trimmings and the heads and shells of the prawns can be reserved and used to make a shellfish-flavoured fish stock.

Spicy Sweet Potatoes
and Peas

Serves 6

Working (and total) time: about 30 minutes

Calories 130, Protein 2g, Cholesterol 5mg, Total fat 6g,
Saturated fat 2g, Sodium 100mg

600 g/1¼ lb	*sweet potatoes, peeled and cut into 1 cm (½ inch) cubes*
2 tsp	*honey*
3 tbsp	*cider vinegar*
¾ tsp	*chilli powder*
½ tsp	*cinnamon*
1½ tbsp	*safflower oil*
175 g/6 oz	*onion, chopped*
15 g/½ oz	*unsalted butter*
¼ tsp	*salt*
125 g/4 oz	*shelled fresh or frozen peas*

In a small bowl, mix together the honey, 2 tablespoons of the vinegar, the chilli powder and cinnamon. Set the honey mixture aside.

Heat the oil in a large, heavy frying pan over medium-low heat. Add the sweet potatoes and cook, stirring occasionally, for 5 minutes. Raise the heat to medium high and cook for another 5 minutes, stirring frequently to prevent the sweet potatoes from sticking. Add the onion, butter, salt, the remaining vinegar and 6 cl (2 fl oz) of water. If you are using fresh peas, add them at this point. Cook, stirring constantly, until the onion just begins to brown—about 5 minutes.

Pour the honey mixture over the vegetables; if you are using frozen peas, stir them in now. Cook the vegetables, stirring constantly, for another 2 minutes and then transfer them to a serving dish.

Fiery Chick-Peas

Serves 14

Working time: about 20 minutes

Total time: about 2 hours and 30 minutes (includes soaking)

Calories 175, Protein 7g, Cholesterol 0mg, Total fat 9g, Saturated fat 1g, Sodium 40mg

500 g/1 lb *dried chick-peas*
6 tbsp *virgin olive oil*
1 *garlic clove*
1 tsp *cayenne pepper*
¹/₄ tsp *salt*

Rinse the chick-peas under cold running water. Put them in a large, heavy-bottomed saucepan and pour in enough cold water to cover them by about 5 cm (2 inches). Discard any chick-peas that float to the surface. Cover the pan, leaving the lid ajar, and bring the water to the boil; cook the chick-peas for 2 minutes. Turn off the heat, cover the pan, and leave the chick-peas to soak for at least 1 hour. (Alternatively, soak the chick-peas overnight in cold water.)

When the chick-peas finish soaking, drain them well in a colander. Return them to the pan and pour in enough water to cover them by about 5 cm (2 inches). Bring the liquid to a simmer, and cook the chick-peas over medium-low heat until they are quite tender—45 minutes to 1 hour. (If they appear to be drying out at any point, pour in more water.) When cooked, drain the chick-peas and allow them to cool.

Dry the chick-peas thoroughly on paper towels or a clean tea towel. Heat the oil in a heavy frying pan until shimmering. Toss in the chick-peas, stir around for a few seconds, then add the garlic.

Reduce the heat to medium and sauté the chick-peas, stirring and tossing from time to time, until their skins are golden-brown—20 to 25 minutes. If the chick-peas pop and jump, either reduce the heat slightly or cover the pan.

Tip the chick-peas on to multiple thicknesses of paper towels and roll them around to remove as much oil as possible. While still hot, put them in a bowl, add the cayenne pepper and salt, and toss well. Serve the chick-peas warm, to be eaten with the fingers.

Butterflying a Prawn

1 CUTTING THE UNDERSHELL. Remove and discard the head of the prawn and gently pull off the legs. Using small kitchen scissors, cut the undershell of the prawn along its length.

2 SLITTING THE PRAWN. Using a sharp knife, slit open the prawn; cut right through the prawn to its shell without splitting the shell. Remove the intestinal tract running down the back of the prawn and discard.

3 OPENING OUT THE PRAWN. Lay the prawn on the work surface, cut side down. Press hard with your fingers along the spine of the shell until it cracks. Alternatively, slit the prawn and shell lengthwise, leaving 1 cm (¹/₂ inch) intact in the centre of the spine, and push the cut ends apart for a full butterfly effect.

Ginger-Spiced Prawns

Makes 12 prawns
Working time: about 30 minutes
Total time: about 2 hours and 30 minutes
(includes marinating)
Per prawn: Calories 30, Protein 3g, Cholesterol 20mg,
Total fat 2g, Saturated fat trace, Sodium 30mg

12	*raw Mediterranean prawns (about 500 g/ 1 lb), gutted and butterflied (left)*
4 tbsp	*low-sodium soy sauce or shoyu*
2 tsp	*fresh lemon or lime juice*
2 tsp	*honey*
2.5 cm/1 inch	*piece fresh ginger root, peeled and finely chopped, or the juice extracted with a garlic press*
1	*garlic clove, finely chopped*
¹/₂ tsp	*Chinese five-spice powder*
1 tbsp	*light sesame oil*
	lettuce leaves, washed, dried and shredded for garnish
	lemon wedges, for garnish (optional)

Combine the soy sauce, lemon or lime juice, honey ginger, garlic and five-spice powder in a wide, shallow non-reactive dish. Place the butterflied prawns in this mixture, flesh side down, and leave to marinate in a cool place for 2 hours.

Preheat the grill to high, and brush a wide, fireproof pan with 1 teaspoon of the oil. Reserving the marinade, place the prawns, flesh side down, in the pan. Brush the shells of the prawns with the remaining oil and grill for 3 to 5 minutes, turning once, until the shells turn pink and the flesh is no longer translucent.

Meanwhile, reduce the reserved marinade in a small saucepan over high heat until only 1 tablespoon remains. Brush this glaze over both sides of the prawns. Serve immediately on a bed of the shredded lettuce, accompanied, if you like, with lemon wedges.

Ginger-Stirred
Vegetables in Pitta

Serves 4

Working (and total) time: about 20 minutes

Calories 165, Protein 5g, Cholesterol 0mg, Total fat 5g,
Saturated fat 1g, Sodium 390mg

2	*large pittas, or four small pittas*
1 tbsp	*light sesame oil*
1	*small garlic clove, crushed*
2	*2.5 cm (1 inch) pieces fresh ginger root, peeled*
60 g/2 oz	*fresh shiitake mushrooms, sliced, or 30 g (1 oz) dried shiitake mushrooms, soaked, drained and sliced*
100 g/3½ oz	*baby sweetcorn, sliced*
250 g/8 oz	*courgettes, julienned*
1 tbsp	*fresh lemon juice*
1 tsp	*tamari, or 1 tsp shoyu mixed with ½ tsp honey*
¼ tsp	*salt*
	freshly ground black pepper

Wrap the pittas in paper towels and microwave on high for 30 seconds. Cut large pittas in half crosswise or, if using small ones, cut them open along one side.

Place the oil and garlic in a wide, shallow dish. Using a garlic press, squeeze the juice from one piece of ginger, and shred the second piece very finely. Add the ginger juice and shreds to the oil.

Microwave the oil and flavourings on high for 30 seconds. Add the mushrooms to the dish, cover with plastic film, leaving a corner open, and microwave on medium for 2 minutes. Add the sweetcorn, re-cover the dish, leaving a corner open as before, and microwave for a further 2 minutes on medium. Then add the courgettes to the mushrooms and sweetcorn and microwave, uncovered, on high for 1 minute. Season with the lemon juice, tamari or shoyu and honey, salt andsomefreshlygroundpepper, and divide the mixture among the pitta pockets.

Arrange the pittas on paper towels or a serving dish in a single layer, evenly spaced. Microwave them on medium for 1½ minutes, rearranging the pittas half way through to ensure even cooking. Serve at once.

Red-Hot Monkfish

Makes about 50 bite-sized pieces
Working time: about 25 minutes
Total time: about 1 hour and 10 minutes
Per piece: Calories 25, Protein 3g, Cholesterol 10mg,
Total fat 1g, Saturated fat trace, Sodium 20mg

1.25 kg/2¹/₂ lb	*ripe tomatoes, roughly chopped, or 800 g/28 oz canned tomatoes, drained*
2¹/₂ tbsp	*virgin olive oil*
1	*small onion, finely chopped*
2	*garlic cloves, crushed*
1	*small sweet green pepper, seeded, deribbed and finely chopped*
15 g/¹/₂ oz	*fresh green chilli pepper, seeded and finely chopped*
¹/₈ tsp	*chilli powder*
1 tsp	*caster sugar*
1 tsp	*Dijon mustard*
1 tsp	*fresh lemon juice*
¹/₄ tsp	*salt*
	freshly ground black pepper
1 kg/2¹/₄ lb	*filleted and skinned monkfish*

Tip the tomatoes into a nylon sieve set over a bowl, and push them through the sieve with a wooden spoon to make a thin purée. Discard the pips and sol-ids that collect in the sieve. Set the purée aside.

Heat ¹/₂ tablespoon of the oil in a heavy-bottomed saucepan and gently sweat the onion until soft but not coloured. Add the garlic and sweet green pepper, stir for a minute or two, then add the chilli, tomato purée, chilli powder, sugar, mustard and lemon juice.

Bring to a vigorous boil then lower the heat and maintain a light boil until the sauce has reduced to about 35 cl (12 fl oz)—about 40 minutes. Add the salt and a little black pepper. Set aside.

Trim the monkfish of any loose membrane and cut it into about fifty 2.5 cm (1 inch) cubes. Heat 1 table-spoon of the remaining oil in a large sauté pan and cook half of the fish pieces for 2 to 3 minutes, until just done. Using a slotted spoon, transfer the fish to the sauce. Clean the pan, add the remaining oil and cook the remaining fish pieces in the same way. Transfer the fish to the sauce and heat through.

Pour a little sauce on to a warm serving dish. Ar-range the monkfish pieces on top and then pour over any remaining sauce. Serve hot with cocktail sticks to spear the fish.

Folding Phyllo Packages

1 MAKING THE FIRST FOLD. Position a strip of phyllo with a short side towards you. Brush the strip lightly with butter. Place a teaspoon of filling on the phyllo about 2 cm (³/4 inch) from the end nearest you. Lift one corner of the strip and fold it over the filling so that the corner meets the opposite long side, creating a triangle.

2 MAKING THE SECOND FOLD. Using both hands, lift the triangle of phyllo containing the filling and fold it away from you.

3 COMPLETING THE PACKAGE. Continue folding the package alternately across and up the strip until you reach the far end, any short band of phyllo remaining at the far end may be trimmed off or folded round the package.

Miniature Samosas

Makes 32 samosas
Working (and total) time: about 1 hour and 15 minutes
Per samosa: Calories 25, Protein 1g, Cholesterol 3mg,
Total fat 1g, Saturated fat 1g, Sodium 35mg

250 g/8 oz	potatoes, peeled and chopped
90 g/3 oz	carrots, sliced
7 g/¹/4 oz	dried ceps, soaked for 20 minutes in hot water
1 tsp	poppy seeds
40 g	unsalted butter
1	small onion, finely chopped
60 g/2 oz	shelled young fresh or frozen peas
1 cm/¹/2 inch	piece fresh ginger root, finely chopped
¹/2 tsp	garam masala
¹/2 tsp	salt
¹/8 tsp	cayenne pepper
4	sheets phyllo pastry, each about 45 by 30 cm (18 by 12 inches) coriander sprigs, for garnish

Coriander-yoghurt dip

15	coriander sprigs, leaves only, finely chopped
¹/4 litre/8 fl oz	plain low-fat yoghurt freshly ground black pepper

Boil the potatoes and carrots separately until they are tender—12 to 15 minutes. Drain and leave to cool. Chop the carrots into small dice and coarsely mash the potatoes. Drain and squeeze dry the ceps, and chop them finely.

Toast the poppy seeds in a dry frying pan until they start to change colour, then remove from the heat.

Melt 7 g (¹/4 oz) of the butter in a heavy frying pan over medium heat and fry the onion until golden-brown. Add the peas, mushrooms and ginger, and cook for 2 to 3 minutes, stirring continuously. Add the potatoes and carrots, and mix well. Remove from the heat, stir in the garam masala, salt and cayenne pepper, and set the filling aside.

Preheat the oven to 200°C (400°F or Mark 6). Cut one sheet of phyllo into eight strips measuring about 30 by 5.5 cm (12 by 2¹/4 inches). Keep the phyllo you are not working on covered with a damp cloth. Melt the remaining butter and lightly brush one side of each phyllo strip, then make up the strips into triangular packages, each enclosing about 1 teaspoon of filling, as demonstrated opposite. Place the phyllo packages on a lightly greased or non-stick baking sheet with the loose ends underneath. Bake in the oven for 15 to 20 minutes, until golden-brown.

To make the dip, mix the coriander into the yoghurt and season with some pepper. Serve the samosas hot, garnished with the coriander sprigs and accompanied by the coriander-yoghurt dip.

Spanish Tortilla Triangles

Serves 8

Working time: about 15 minutes

Total time: about 30 minutes

Calories 100, Protein 4g, Cholesterol 110mg, Total fat 7g,
Saturated fat 2g, Sodium 135mg

2 tbsp	*virgin olive oil*
2	*leeks, trimmed, cleaned and cut diagonally into fine slices*
2	*garlic cloves, finely chopped*
1	*sweet red pepper, seeded, deribbed and finely chopped*
1	*sweet green pepper, seeded, deribbed and finely chopped*
4	*eggs*
1/2 tsp	*salt*
	freshly ground black pepper
250 g/8 oz	*cooked peeled potatoes, chopped*
2 tbsp	*chopped parsley*

Heat 1 1/2 tablespoons of the oil in a heavy frying pan and cook the leeks over low heat until softened—about 10 minutes. Add the garlic and peppers and cook for a further 10 minutes, stirring occasionally.

Mix the eggs in a bowl with the salt and some pepper, then stir in the cooked vegetable mixture, potatoes and parsley. Preheat the grill to high.

Heat the remaining oil in a 22 cm (9 inch) omelette pan and pour in the egg mixture. Cook over low heat for 4 minutes, until the bottom of the omelette is golden-brown—lift gently with a palette knife to check. Place the pan under the grill and cook until the egg is set—about 3 minutes. Slide the omelette on to a plate, cut into eight triangles and serve at once.

Spiced Coconut Crab Dip
with Poppadoms

Serves 8

Working (and total) time: about 30 minutes

Calories 140, Protein 9g, Cholesterol 30mg, Total fat 5g,
Saturated fat 1g, Sodium 260mg

60 g/2 oz	creamed coconut
1/4 litre/8 fl oz	unsalted chicken stock
2.5 cm/1 inch	piece fresh ginger root, peeled and sliced
6	cardamom pods, crushed
1	blade mace
2	chilli peppers, split lengthwise and seeded
1	fresh turmeric root, sliced, or 1/2 teaspoon ground turmeric
1/8 tsp	saffron threads
1	lime or bay leaf
5 tbsp	soured cream
2 tsp	cornflour
1 tsp	dry mustard
2 tbsp	dry sherry
1 tbsp	tomato paste
125 g	white crab meat, picked over
125 g	brown crab meat, picked over
1	tamarillo, peeled, seeded and finely diced
1 tsp	fresh lemon juice
1/2 tsp	salt
1/4 tsp	cayenne pepper, plus a sprinkling, for garnish
16	poppadoms
	finely shredded chilli pepper, for garnish

Blend the creamed coconut with the chicken stock in a bowl. Add the ginger, cardamom, mace, chillies, turmeric, saffron and lime or bay leaf. Microwave on low for 5 minutes, to infuse the liquid with the spices. Strain the coconut mixture through a sieve into a 90 cl (1 1/2 pint) dish, pressing down hard on the spices. Stir in the soured cream and mix well.

In a small bowl, blend the cornflour, mustard powder and sherry, and stir this into the coconut mixture. Then stir in the tomato paste. Microwave the mixture on medium for about 3 minutes, or until the liquid has thickened and begun to bubble.

Stir the white and brown crab meat into the coconut-tomato mixture, and microwave for 30 seconds on medium. Stir in the diced tamarillo and microwave for a further 30 seconds, again on medium. Finally, add the lemon juice, salt and cayenne pepper.

Place four poppadoms at a time in the microwave oven in a single layer on paper towels and cook on high for about 1 minute, rearranging after 30 seconds; the poppadoms are cooked when they appear evenly 'puffed' and no dark patches remain.

Meanwhile, transfer the dip to a serving dish and garnish with a little shredded chilli and a sprinkling of cayenne. Serve at once with the poppadoms.

Spiced Peanut Dip with Crudité Skewers

Serves 10

Working time: about 1 hour and 30 minutes

Total time: about 5 hours (includes chilling)

Calories 105, Protein 5g, Cholesterol 2mg, Total fat 6g, Saturated fat 1g, Sodium 165mg

15 cl/¹/₄ pint	unsalted chicken stock
1 tsp	saffron threads
125 g/4 oz	shelled peanuts
1 tbsp	virgin olive oil
1	large onion, very finely chopped
4	garlic cloves, crushed
30 g/1 oz	fresh ginger root, peeled and sliced
2 tsp	ground coriander
1 tsp	ground cumin
1 tsp	ground cardamom
30 cl/¹/₂ pint	plain low-fat yoghurt
¹/₂ tsp	salt
	freshly ground black pepper
2 tsp	finely cut fresh chives
1 tsp	finely chopped parsley
	Crudité skewers
175 g/6 oz	daikon radish, peeled
175 g/6 oz	radishes, preferably very tiny, trimmed
175 g/6 oz	carrots, peeled
175 g/6 oz	sticks celery, scrubbed
1	small sweet red pepper, seeded and deribbed
1	small sweet green pepper, seeded and deribbed
1	small sweet yellow pepper, seeded and deribbed

1 *small sweet orange pepper, seeded and deribbed (optional)*

Preheat the oven to 220°C (425°F or Mark 7). In a saucepan, heat the chicken stock to boiling point; remove from the heat and add the saffron threads. Stir well and leave to stand for about 30 minutes.

Spread the peanuts out on a small baking sheet, then roast them in the oven for 6 to 8 minutes, until their skins loosen. Rub the nuts in a clean tea towel to remove their skins. Heat the oil in a saucepan; add the onions and cook gently until they are very soft but not browned—8 to 10 minutes. Stir in the garlic.

Put the ginger, coriander, cumin, cardamom, yoghurt, peanuts and saffron mixture into a blender or food processor, and blend until smooth. Pour on to the onions and stir well. Cook over low heat until the mixture thickens—about 20 minutes. Season with the salt and some pepper. Pour into a bowl; cover closely with plastic film to prevent a skin forming. When cool, chill in the refrigerator for 3 to 4 hours, or overnight.

Just before serving, prepare the vegetables. Cut them into decoratively shaped slices, as illustrated here, or into small neat cubes, and thread them on to cocktail sticks. Stir the dip and spoon it into a serving bowl, then sprinkle the top with the chives and parsley. Place the bowl on a large serving platter and surround with the crudité skewers.

EDITOR'S NOTE: If preferred, the vegetables may be cut into 10 cm (4 inch) long sticks, and arranged round the dip.

Thai Skewers

Makes 18 skewers
Working time: about 25 minutes
Total time: about 2 hours and 40 minutes (includes chilling)
Per skewer: Calories 55, Protein 6g, Cholesterol 40mg,
Total fat 2g, Saturated fat trace, Sodium 90mg

250 g/8 oz	pork fillet or escalope, trimmed of fat
350 g/12 oz	raw prawns, shelled and deveined
100 g/3¹/₂ oz	white crab meat, picked over
3	garlic cloves
2.5 cm/1 inch	piece fresh ginger root, peeled
¹/₂ tsp	fresh lime juice
¹/₄ tsp	grated lime rind
1 tsp	ground galangal
1 tsp	ground lemon grass
3 tbsp	chopped fresh coriander
1 tbsp	chopped fresh basil
¹/₂ tsp	salt
	freshly ground black pepper
1 tsp	arrowroot
¹/₂	beaten egg white
1	papaya, peeled and cut into 1cm (¹/₂ inch) cubes
1 tbsp	safflower oil

Aromatic dip

2 tbsp	low-sodium soy sauce or shoyu
1 tbsp	fresh lime juice
1 tbsp	molasses sugar
1	garlic clove
1 cm/¹/₂ inch	piece fresh ginger root, peeled
	fine strips of fresh chilli pepper

Mince the pork finely in a food processor, then transfer it to a large bowl. Process the prawns to a fine paste and add them to the minced pork, then process and add the white crab meat. Mix the pork and shellfish together well with your hands.

Using a garlic press, squeeze the juice from the garlic and ginger into the pork and shellfish mixture. Add the lime juice and rind, galangal, lemon grass, coriander, basil, salt and a generous grinding of black pepper. Mix the ingredients together. Stir the arrowroot into the egg white until no lumps remain, and blend the arrowroot and egg white into the pork and fish mixture. Chill for at least 2 hours.

To make the dip, combine the soy sauce and lime juice with 2 tablespoons of water in a small bowl, and dissolve the molasses sugar in the mixture. Using a garlic press, squeeze the juice from the garlic and fresh ginger into the mixture. Add the chilli peppers and pour into a serving bowl.

Preheat the grill to medium. Soak 18 wooden satay sticks or skewers in water for about 10 minutes to prevent them from burning under the grill.

Form the chilled pork and shellfish mixture into 54 small balls, each about 2 cm (³/₄ inch) in diameter. Thread three balls on to each skewer, alternating them with cubes of papaya.

Brush a grill pan lightly with a little of the safflower oil, and arrange the skewers in a single layer in the pan. Brush the balls and the papaya cubes lightly with the remaining oil. Cook the skewers for about 10 minutes, turning once, until they are golden-brown. Serve immediately, accompanied by the dip.

Thai-Style Parcels

THE INGREDIENTS FOR THIS DISH ARE PREPARED BY THE COOK AND
PRESENTED AT THE TABLE FOR EACH GUEST TO ASSEMBLE INDIVIDUALLY.

Makes 48 parcels
Working time about 1 hour
Total time: about 4 hours (includes chilling and marinating)
Per parcel: Calories 30, Protein 3g, Cholesterol 10mg,
Total fat 2g, Saturated fat 1g, Sodium 25mg

350 g/12 oz	*lean fillet of beef, trimmed of fat and chilled in the freezer until firm (about 1 hour)*
350 g/12 oz	*boneless chicken breast, skinned*
1	*Chinese cabbage, washed, dried and finely shredded*
1	*large lettuce, leaves washed and dried*
1/2	*cucumber, peeled in alternate strips with a cannelle knife, halved lengthwise and thinly sliced*
1	*bunch fresh coriander, leaves only*
1	*bunch fresh mint, large stalks removed*
1	*bunch fresh basil, leaves only*
48	*rice-paper wrappers (about 6 inches/15 cm in diameter)*
1 tbsp	*groundnut oil*
	freshly ground black pepper

Spicy marinade

30 g/1 oz	*tamarind paste, dissolved in 15 cl (1/4 pint) water for 15 minutes*
1 tsp	*sambal oelek*
1 tbsp	*ketjap manis or low-sodium soy sauce*
2 tsp	*nam pla, or 1 tsp anchovy purée*
3	*garlic cloves, crushed*
4 cm/1 1/2 inch	*piece fresh ginger root, peeled and finely shredded*

Lemon glaze

4 tbsp	*fresh lemon juice*
2 tbsp	*ketjap manis or low sodium soy sauce*
1 tsp	*molasses sugar*

Dipping sauce

10 cl/3 1/2 fl oz	*fresh lemon juice*
4 tbsp	*ketjap manis or low-sodium soy sauce*
2 tsp	*sambal oelek*
1 cm/1/2 inch	*piece fresh ginger root, peeled and finely shredded*
1	*small stick fresh lemon grass, finely chopped*

To make the marinade, strain the tamarind liquid and discard the solids. Add the sambal oelek, ketjap manis, nam pla, garlic and ginger to the liquid and stir well to blend the ingredients. Divide the marinade between two shallow dishes. Slice the beef very thinly across the grain, then cut the slices into strips about 1 cm (1/2 inch) wide. Cut the chicken breast into thin strips of the same width. Place the beef in one of the marinade dishes, and the chicken in the other; stir to coat the strips evenly, and leave to marinate in a cool place for 3 hours.

Shortly before serving, combine the glaze ingredients with 2 tablespoons of water in a small saucepan and boil until reduced to about 3 tablespoons—3 to 5 minutes.

Meanwhile, make up the dipping sauce by combining all the ingredients with 4 tablespoons of water. Pour the sauce into dipping bowls. Arrange the Chinese cabbage, lettuce leaves and cucumber slices on a serving platter, and the coriander, mint and basil on a second platter. Set out the rice-paper wrappers and bowls of tepid water for dipping the wrappers.

In a wok or a wide, heavy frying pan, heat the oil until sizzling. Take the beef strips out of the marinade and sear them for about 20 seconds, stirring and tossing the meat with a spatula. Remove the beef and keep warm. Cook the chicken strips in the wok until the flesh is no longer translucent—about 45 seconds.

Arrange the beef and chicken on separate serving dishes, and brush with the glaze. Serve immediately, with the raw ingredients, pepper and sauce, for each guest to make up into parcels and dip.

Potato, Carrot and Cauliflower Curry

Serves 6
Working time: about 30 minutes
Total time: about 1 hour
Calories 230, Protein 6g, Cholesterol 0mg, Total fat 11g, Saturated fat 5g, Sodium 230mg

2 tbsp *virgin olive oil*
2 *onions, finely chopped*
60 g/2 oz *fresh ginger root, peeled and grated*
3 *garlic cloves, crushed*
2 *fresh hot green chilli peppers, seeded and finely chopped*
2 tsp *paprika*
1/2 tsp *ground tumeric*
1 tsp *ground cumin*
45 cl/³/4 pint *unsalted vegetable stock*
500 g/1 lb *potatoes, cut into 1 cm (¹/2 inch) dice*
250 g/8 oz *carrots, cut into 1 cm (¹/2 inch) dice*
250 g/8 oz *cauliflower florets*
175 g/6 oz *French beans, trimmed and cut into 2.5 cm (1 inch) lengths*
175 g/6 oz *shelled peas, or frozen peas, thawed*
90 g/3 oz *coconut milk powder or creamed coconut, blended with 12.5 cl (4 fl oz) warm water*
1 tbsp *cornflour, blended with 3 tbsp cold water*
1/2 tsp *salt*
freshly ground black pepper

Put the olive oil and onions into a large bowl. Microwave on high, uncovered, for 5 to 6 minutes, until the onions are softened, stirring half way through the cooking time. Stir in the ginger, garlic, chillies, paprika, turmeric and cumin and cook on high, uncovered, for 2 minutes. Add the stock, potatoes, carrots and cauliflower and stir well, then cover the bowl with plastic film, pulling back one corner to allow steam to escape. Cook on high for 20 minutes, stirring every 5 minutes. Then stir in the beans and peas and cook, covered as before, for a further 10 minutes, until the vegetables are tender.

Stir the coconut milk and cornflour mixtures into the vegetables and cook, uncovered, on high for 5 minutes, stirring half way through. Season with the salt and some black pepper. Allow the curry to stand for 5 minutes before serving.

Tandoori Patties

Serves 4
Working time: about 45 minutes
Total time about 2 hours and 45 minutes
(includes soaking)
Calories 305, Protein 14g, Cholesterol 0mg, Total fat 6g,
Saturated fat 1g, Sodium 290mg

250 g/8 oz	*dried pinto beans, picked over*
1 tbsp	*safflower oil*
1	*onion, chopped*
2	*garlic cloves, chopped*
3 tsp	*tandoori spice*
1 tsp	*ground cumin*
30 g/1 oz	*fresh wholemeal breadcrumbs*
2 tbsp	*chopped fresh coriander*
2 tbsp	*tomato paste*
125 g/4 oz	*parsnips or carrots, finely grated*
1/2 tsp	*salt*
	freshly ground black pepper
3 tbsp	*wholemeal flour*
1 tsp	*paprika*

Coriander-yoghurt sauce

15 cl/1/4 pint	*plain low-fat yoghurt*
1/2 tsp	*ground coriander*
1 tsp	*tomato paste*
1	*garlic clove, crushed*
2 tsp'	*chopped fresh coriander*

Rinse the beans under cold running water, put them into a large, heavy pan, and pour in enough cold water to cover them by about 7.5 cm (3 inches). Discard any beans that float to the surface. Cover the pan, leaving the lid ajar, and slowly bring the liquid to the boil. Boil the beans for 2 minutes, then turn off the heat and soak the beans, covered, for at least 1 hour. (Alternatively, soak the beans overnight in cold water.)

Rinse the beans, place them in a clean saucepan, and pour in enough water to cover them by about 7.5 cm (3 inches). Bring the liquid to the boil. Boil the beans for 10 minutes, then drain and rinse them again. Wash out the pan, replace the beans and again pour in enough water to cover them by about 7.5 cm (3 inches). Bring the liquid to the boil, reduce the heat to maintain a strong simmer, cover the pan, and cook the beans until they are tender—about 1 hour. Check the water level in the pan from time to time and pour in more hot water if the beans appear to be drying out. Drain the cooked beans in a colander, rinse them under cold running water and set them aside.

Heat 1/2 tablespoon of the oil in a heavy frying pan and fry the onion over medium heat for about 3 minutes, until soft. Add the chopped garlic, 2 teaspoons of the tandoori spice and the ground cumin, and fry for a further minute.

Put the onion mixture and the beans into a food processor or blender with the breadcrumbs, fresh coriander, tomato paste, parsnips or carrots, salt and some pepper. Blend until smooth, scraping down the sides of the processor bowl as necessary.

Preheat the grill to medium high. Mix the flour with the remaining tandoori spice and the paprika. Dampen your hands and shape the blended mixture into eight balls, then flatten the balls into patties. Roll the patties in the spiced flour to coat them. Brush the patties with the remaining oil and grill them for 3 to 4 minutes on each side, until they are crisp.

Meanwhile, mix all the sauce ingredients together. Serve the patties hot, with the coriander-yoghurt sauce.

EDITOR'S NOTE: Tandoori spice, a curry powder containing coriander, chilli, ginger, turmeric, fenugreek, garlic and other spices, is used in Indian cuisine to flavour food baked in a "tandoor"; a clay oven.

Oven-Fried Cinnamon Chicken

Serves 4
Working time: about 15 minutes
Total time: about 1 hour
Calories 425, Protein 47g, Cholesterol 125mg, Total fat
17g, Saturated fat 3g, Sodium 565g

1.5 kg/3 lb	*chicken, quartered and skinned*
1/2 tsp	*salt*
1/2 tsp	*freshly ground white pepper*
4 tbsp	*plain flour*
1/4 tsp	*turmeric*
1 tsp	*cinnamon*
3	*egg whites*
60 g/2 oz	*fresh breadcrumbs*
2 tbsp	*safflower oil*

Preheat the oven to 170°C (325°F or Mark 3). Mix the salt, pepper and flour, and spread on a plate. In a small bowl, whisk the turmeric and cinnamon into the egg whites. Dredge the chicken pieces in the flour, then dip them in the egg whites and coat them with the breadcrumbs.

In a fireproof pan or shallow casserole large enough to hold the chicken pieces in a single layer, heat the oil over medium heat. Lay the pieces bone side up in the pan and brown them lightly on one side—about 2 minutes. Turn the pieces over, put the pan in the oven, and bake for 30 minutes.

Remove the pan and increase the oven temperature to 230°C (450°F or Mark 8). Wait about 5 minutes, then return to the oven and let the coating crisp for 4 or 5 minutes, taking care not to burn it.

Turkey and Green Chilli Enchiladas

IN MEXICAN COOKING, ENCHILADAS ARE FILLED TORTILLAS SERVED WITH A SAUCE.

Serves 4

Working time: about 40 minutes

Total time: about 1 hour

Calories 455, Protein 38g, Cholesterol 70mg, Total fat 16g, Saturated fat 4g, Sodium 375mg

350 g/12 oz	cooked turkey meat, shredded or slivered
2 to 5	fresh hot green chili peppers, seeded, finely chopped
1	large onion, coarsely chopped
1	large tomato, cored, seeded and coarsely chopped
2	garlic cloves, coarsely chopped
2 tbsp	chopped fresh coriander
4 tbsp	unsalted turkey or chicken stock
2 tbsp	fresh lemon juice
1/8 tbsp	sugar
350 g/12 oz	tomatillos, papery husks removed, blanched 2 minutes, cored and quartered
90 g/3 oz	mild Cheddar cheese, grated
1/2 tsp	ground cumin
1 tsp	chopped fresh oregano, or 1/4 tsp dried oregano
1/8 tsp	salt
8	corn tortillas (canned or freshly made)
12.5 cl/4 fl oz	soured cream
12.5 cl/4 fl oz	plain low-fat yoghurt

Preheat the oven to 180°C (350°F or Mark 4). Scrape three quarters of the chilies into a food processor or blender. Add the onion, tomato, garlic, coriander, stock, lemon juice and sugar. Using short bursts, process the mixture into a rough purée—about 8 seconds. Add the tomatillos and process until coarsely chopped—about 5 seconds. Pour the sauce into a saucepan and simmer it over medium heat for 10 minutes.

Next, make the filling for the tortillas. In a large bowl, combine the turkey, 60 g (2 oz) of the cheese, the remaining hot chilies, the cumin, oregano, salt and half of the sauce.

Place a heavy frying pan over medium heat. Warm a tortilla in the pan for 10 seconds on each side to soften it, then place it in the hot sauce, carefully turn it over, and transfer it to a plate. Spoon about 5 tablespoons of the turkey filling down the centre of the tortilla, then roll it up to enclose the filling, and place it seam side down in a large oiled baking dish. Fill the remaining tortillas.

Pour the rest of the hot sauce over the enchiladas and sprinkle them with the remaining cheese. Bake, uncovered, for 20 minutes. Meanwhile, combine the soured cream and yoghurt as a topping; spoon it over the enchiladas just before serving them.

EDITOR'S NOTE: The tomatillos called for in this recipe are also known as Mexican ground cherries and are closely related to the Cape gooseberry. If they are unavailable, substitute 350 g (12 oz) of fresh green unripe tomatoes, coarsely chopped.

Turkey Curry with Puréed Yams

Serves 6

Working time: about 30 minutes

Total time: about 1 hour 45 minutes

Calories 335, Protein 25g, Cholesterol 75 mg, Total fat
12g, Saturated fat 6g, Sodium 255mg

600 g/1¼ lb	*boneless dark turkey meat, skinned and cut into 2.5 cm (1 inch) cubes*
45 g/1½ oz	*unsalted butter*
2	*small yams or sweet potatoes, peeled and cut into 1 cm(½ inch) cubes*
¾ litre/1¼ pints	*unsalted turkey or chicken stock*
2	*medium onions, finely chopped*
1	*stick celery, finely chopped*
2	*garlic cloves. finely chopped*
½ tsp	*grated fresh ginger root, or ¼ tsp ground ginger*
½ tsp	*fresh thyme, or ⅛ tsp dried thyme*
2 tbsp	*curry powder*
5 tbsp	*fresh lemon juice*
¼ tsp	*salt*
	freshly ground black pepper
60 g/2 oz	*sultanas*
150 g/5 oz	*peas*

In a saucepan, bring 1 litre (1¾ pints) of water to the boil. Add the turkey, blanch for 1 minute, and drain.

In a large, heavy frying pan over low heat, melt half of the butter Add the yams and cook them slowly, stirring frequently, until they are browned and tender—about 25 minutes. Purée the yams with ¼ litre (8 fl oz) of stock in a food processor or blender, and set them aside.

Over medium-low heat, melt the remaining butter in the frying pan. Add the onions, celery. garlic, ginger and thyme. Cook, stirring frequently, until the onions begin to brown—about 15 minutes.

Add the turkey, curry powder, lemon juice, salt and pepper. Reduce the heat to low and gently stir in the rest of the stock. Cover and simmer for 45 minutes. Uncover the frying pan and add the sultanas and the yam purée. Cover the pan again and cook, stirring occasionally, until the turkey cubes are tender—about 30 minutes more. Add the peas and cook another 5 minutes. Serve the curry immediately.

Sichuan Stir-Fried Veal and Crunchy Vegetables

Serves 4

Working time: about 40 minutes

Total time: about 2 hours and 40 minutes
(includes marinating)

Calories 300, Protein 30g, Cholesterol 110mg, Total fat
14g, Saturated fat 3g, Sodium 215mg

500 g/1 lb	*veal escalopes, trimmed of fat, flattened and cut diagonally into strips 4 cm(1½ inches) long by 5 mm (¼ inch) wide*
4 tbsp	*low-sodium soy sauce or shoyu*
4 tbsp	*sake or dry sherry*
2	*dried red chili peppers, finely chopped*
2 tbsp	*safflower oil*
6	*spring onions, sliced diagonally*
2.5 cm/1 inch	*fresh ginger root, cut into very fine julienne*
1 to 2	*garlic cloves, crushed*
125 g/4 oz	*whole baby sweet corns*
250 g/8 oz	*carrots, julienned*
125 g/4 oz	*cauliflower florets*
125 g/4 oz	*French beans, topped and tailed*
30 cl/½ pint	*unsalted chicken or veal stock*
1 tbsp	*tomato paste*
1½ tbsp	*cornflour, mixed with 1 tbsp cold water freshly ground black pepper*
1 tbsp	*sesame oil*

In a bowl, combine the strips of veal, 2 tablespoons each of the soy sauce and sake, and the chilies. Cover and leave to marinate for 2 hours, turning occasionally.

Heat a wok or a large, deep, heavy frying pan over medium-high heat and pour in the safflower oil. Add the spring onions, ginger and garlic, and stir-fry for 30 seconds to flavour the oil. Add the veal and its marinade and stir-fry, tossing frequently, until all the strips have changed colour—about 3 minutes. Remove the veal and flavourings with a slotted spoon and set aside on a plate; do not discard the oil.

Add the baby sweetcorn to the pan and stir-fry, tossing constantly, for 2 minutes, then add the carrots, cauliflower and beans, and stir-fry for a further 2 minutes. Return the veal and flavourings to the pan and stir-fry to combine with the vegetables. Push the contents to the sides and pour the stock into the centre. Stir in the tomato paste, remaining soy sauce and sake, the cornflour mixture and some pepper. Bring to the boil and boil until the liquid thickens—1 to 2 minutes. Redistribute the veal and vegetables in the sauce and stir to coat all the pieces evenly.

Serve the veal and vegetables with the sesame oil sprinkled over the top.

Spicy Beef Stew
with Apricots and Olives

Serves 8
Working time: about 30 minutes
Total time: about 2 hours and 30 minutes
Calories 290, Protein 29g, Cholesterol 70mg, Total fat 11g,
Saturated fat 3g, Sodium 275mg

1.25 kg/2¹/₂ lb	topside of beef, trimmed of fat and cut into 4 cm(1¹/₂ inch) cubes
1 tbsp	safflower oil
3	onions, chopped
4	garlic cloves, finely chopped
400 g/14 oz	canned whole tomatoes, chopped, with their juice
¹/₂ litre/16 fl oz	unsalted brown or chicken stock
12.5 cl/4 fl oz	red wine
1¹/₂ tsp	ground cumin
1¹/₂ tsp	ground coriander
¹/₈ tsp	cayenne pepper
125 g/4 oz	dried apricots, halved
16	green olives, stoned, rinsed and drained

Heat the oil in a large, heavy frying pan over medium heat. Add the onions and cook them, stirring often, until translucent—about 5 minutes. With a slotted spoon, transfer the onions to a fireproof casserole.

Increase the heat to medium high. Add the beef cubes to the frying pan and brown them on all sides—5 to 7 minutes.

Transfer the beef to the casserole and add the garlic, the tomatoes and their juice, the stock, wine, cumin, coriander and cayenne pepper. Cover the casserole and reduce the heat to low; simmer the beef, stirring occasionally, for 1¹/₂ hours.

Stir the apricots and olives into the casserole, and continue cooking the stew until the meat is tender—about 30 minutes more. Transfer the stew to a bowl or a deep platter, and serve.

54

Spicy Minced Meat on a Bed of Sweet Potatoes

Serves 4

Working time: about 1 hour

Total time: about 2 hours and 30 minutes

Calories 522, Protein 35g, Cholesterol 75mg, Total fat
10g, Saturated fat 3g, Sodium 260mg

600 g/1¼ lb	topside of beef, trimmed of fat and minced
4	orange-fleshed sweet potatoes (about 1.1 kg/2¼ lb)
1.5 kg/3 lb	ripe tomatoes, chopped
2	bay leaves
2	cinnamon sticks
4	allspice berries
8	black peppercorns
2	dried red chili peppers, or ¼ tsp cayenne pepper
1 tbsp	tomato paste
1 tsp	safflower oil
1	onion, finely chopped
¼ tsp	salt
2 tbsp	chopped parsley
12.5 cl/4 fl oz	plain low-fat yoghurt

Preheat the oven 200°C (400°F or Mark 6). Bake the sweet potatoes for 1 hour or until they are tender when pierced with the tip of a sharp knife.

Meanwhile, put the tomatoes, bay leaves, cinnamon sticks, allspice berries, peppercorns, and chili peppers or cayenne pepper into a heavy, non-reactive pan.

Bring the mixture to the boil, then reduce the heat to medium low, and simmer it uncovered, stirring frequently, until it is reduced to 1½ litre (16 fl oz)—about 1½ hours. Remove the cinnamon sticks and bay leaves from the tomato sauce, discard them, and put the sauce through a sieve. Set the sauce aside.

Sauté the beef in a large, non-stick frying pan over high heat, breaking it into chunks as it cooks. When the beef is evenly browned—about 5 minutes—add the tomato sauce and the tomato paste. Simmer the meat, partially covered to prevent splattering, until most of the liquid has evaporated—about 20 minutes. Pour the meat sauce into a bowl and keep it warm.

Peel the baked sweet potatoes and chop them coarsely. Wipe out the frying pan with a paper towel, pour in the oil and heat it over low heat. Add the onion and cook it until it is translucent—about 5 minutes. Add the sweet potatoes and 4 tablespoons of water, and cook the mixture, stirring frequently, over medium heat until the water is absorbed—about 5 minutes; stir in the salt and chopped parsley.

Place the sweet potatoes on a serving platter and top them with the meat. Serve immediately, passing the yoghurt separately.

Veal and Apricot Brochettes
Tikka-Style

Serves 4

Working time: about 30 minutes

Total time: about 6 hours and 45 minutes

(includes marinating)

Calories 180, Protein 20g, Cholesterol 75mg, Total fat 5g,
Saturated fat 2g, Sodium 240mg

350 g/12 oz	veal topside, top rump or boned loin, trimmed of fat and cut into 2.5 cm (1 inch) cubes
60 g/2 oz	ready-to-eat dried apricots (about 8),halved
250 g/8 oz	courgettes, trimmed and cut into chunks lime wedges or slices for garnish
	Spicy yoghurt marinade
30 cl/¹/₂ pint	plain low-fat yoghurt
1	small onion, chopped
1	garlic clove, chopped
1 cm/¹/₂ inch	fresh ginger root, peeled, or 1 tbsp freshly grated ginger root
1	lime, juice only
2	cardamom pods
1	small dried red chili pepper
4	cloves
6	black peppercorns
5 mm/¹/₄ inch	piece cinnamon stick
1	piece of nutmeg, about the size of a hazelnut, or 1 tsp freshly grated nutmeg
¹/₄ tsp	coriander seeds
¹/₄ tsp	cumin seeds
¹/₄ tsp	salt

Combine the yoghurt, onion, garlic, ginger and lime juice in a food processor and blend until quite smooth. Strain into a bowl.

Break open the cardamom pods and put the seeds in a mortar. Add the chili pepper, cloves, peppercorns, cinnamon stick, nutmeg, coriander seeds and cumin seeds. Pound with a pestle until fine. Alternatively, the spices may be worked in a spice grinder. Add the spices and the salt to the yoghurt mixture and stir well. Add the cubes of veal and the apricots, and coat them in the mixture. Cover and leave to marinate in the refrigerator for at least 6 hours, stirring occasionally.

Preheat the grill. Thread the veal cubes, apricots and courgettes on to four or eight skewers, shaking off and reserving excess marinade. Grill the kebabs for about 15 minutes, turning them to cook and brown evenly.

While the kebabs are cooking, strain the marinade through a fine sieve into a small, heavy-bottomed saucepan. Heat the marinade through very gently, stirring occasionally; do not boil. Serve the kebabs garnished with lime wedges or slices and pass the heated marinade sauce separately.

Veal Steaks Teriyaki

This recipe is based on the Japanese "Teriyaki" style of marinating meat in a mixture of mirin, soy sauce and fresh ginger. The long marinating tenderizes the meat, with succulent results.

Serves 6

Working time: about 10 minutes

Total time: about 25 hours (includes marinating)

Calories 185, Protein 26g, Cholesterol 90mg, Total fat 7g, Saturated fat 2g, Sodium 150mg

500 g/1 lb	veal fillet in one piece, cut diagonally into eight pieces
6 cl/2 fl oz	low-sodium soy sauce or shoyu
2 tbsp	mirin (Japanese sweet rice wine) or sweet sherry
30 g/1 oz	fresh ginger root, peeled and finely chopped
4	garlic cloves, crushed
1 tsp	soft brown sugar
1 tbsp	groundnut oil
1/4 pint/15 cl	unsalted chicken stock
	spring onions or celery cut into brushes for garnish

In a jug, whisk the soy sauce with the mirin or sherry, ginger, garlic and sugar. Put the pieces of veal in a shallow dish and pour over the marinade. Turn the veal several times to ensure that the pieces are evenly coated. Cover and leave to marinate in the refrigerator for 24 to 36 hours, turning the meat occasionally. Thirty minutes before cooking, remove the veal from the refrigerator and let it come to room temperature. Ten minutes before cooking, preheat the grill.

Remove the veal from the marinade, brushing off and reserving any excess marinade. Brush the veal on both sides with the oil, then place the veal on the grill rack. Grill for 3 to 4 minutes, turn and grill for another 3 to 4 minutes.

Meanwhile, transfer the marinade to a small saucepan and add the stock. Bring the liquid to the boil, skim it, then simmer gently. Serve the veal steaks hot with the sauce poured over, garnished with spring onion or celery brushes.

Potatoes with a Spiced Lamb Stuffing

Serves 4

Working time: about 40 minutes

Total time: about 1 hour and 40 minutes

Calories 270, Protein 14g, Cholesterol 25mg, Total fat 5g,
Saturated fat 2g, Sodium 230mg

150 g/5 oz	*lean lamb (from the leg), trimmed of fat and minced*
8	*even-sized potatoes (about 100g/3¹/₂ oz each), scrubbed*
1	*small onion, finely chopped*
1	*garlic clove, crushed*
1 tbsp	*raisins, rinsed and finely chopped*
1 tbsp	*pine-nuts, roughly chopped*
1 tsp	*ground cinnamon*
¹/₂ tsp	*ground allspice*
¹/₂ tsp	*ground turmeric*
2 tbsp	*tomato paste*
¹/₄ tsp	*salt*
	freshly ground black pepper
6 tbsp	*unsalted brown or chicken stock*
1 tbsp	*crème fraîche*

Preheat the oven to 200°C (400°F or Mark 6).

Make a 1 cm (¹/₂ inch) deep horizontal slit about one quarter of the way down each potato Bake them in the oven until they are tender—about 1 hour.

Meanwhile, make the stuffing. Lightly brush a non-stick frying pan with oil and heat it over medium heat. Stir-fry the onion until it is brown—about 5 minutes. Add the minced lamb and continue stir-frying until it changes colour—3 to 4 minutes—then add the garlic, raisins, pine-nuts, cinnamon, allspice, turmeric, tomato paste, salt and some freshly ground pepper. Stir for 1 minute, then add the stock and continue cooking the mixture for a further 5 minutes, stirring regularly. Set the stuffing aside.

When the potatoes are cool enough to handle, slice off their tops and hollow out their insides with a teaspoon, taking care not to puncture their skins; leave a shell of about 5 mm (¹/₄ inch) on each potato. Mash half of the scooped-out potato with the crème fraîche. (Reserve the remaining potato and the tops for another use.) Spoon the mashed potato into the potato shells, pressing down in the centre to make a well for the lamb stuffing. Fill the shells with the stuffing and return them to the oven to heat through—about 10 minutes. Serve immediately.

Sichuan Peppercorn Lamb

Serves 4

Working time: about 30 minutes

Total time: about 45 minutes

Calories 290, Protein 32g, Cholesterol 80mg, Total fat 14g, Saturated fat 5g, Sodium 135mg

4	loin chops (about 150g/5 oz each), trimmed of fat
2 tsp	Sichuan peppercorns
1 tbsp	shoyu or low-sodium soy sauce
1 tbsp	dry sherry
125 g/4 oz	French beans, topped and tailed, cut in half
1/2 tbsp	safflower oil
1 tbsp	finely chopped spring onions
1	large carrot, peeled and julienned
1	sweet red pepper, seeded, deribbed and julienned
	green ends of spring onions, sliced diagonally, for garnish

Heat a heavy-bottomed pan over medium heat and toast the peppercorns by stirring them until their aroma increases—about 30 seconds. Grind them to a fine powder with a mortar and pestle, then mix 1 teaspoon of ground peppercorns together with the shoyu and sherry in a shallow dish. Place the chops in the dish, turn them to coat them and leave to marinate for 20 minutes; turn them once during this time.

Meanwhile, parboil the French beans in boiling water for 3 minutes. Drain and rinse them under cold running water. Drain again and set them aside. Preheat the grill to high.

Remove the chops from the dish and discard the marinade. Dust the chops with the remaining crushed peppercorns, and pin the flap of lean meat to the eye of each chop with a cocktail stick. Grill the chops for 4 to 6 minutes on each side for rare to medium meat.

While the chops are cooking, stir-fry the vegetables. In a wok or heavy frying pan, heat the oil until it is hot but not smoking. Add the chopped spring onions and fry them for 30 seconds, stirring constantly, then add the julienned carrot and pepper, and the beans. Stir fry all the vegetables for 2 minutes, then serve them immediately alongside the grilled chops. Garnish the chops with the spring onion slices.

Pork Vindaloo

Serves 8

Working time: about 15 minutes

Total time: about 26 hours (includes marinating)

Calories 200, Protein 22g, Cholesterol 70mg, Total fat
10g, Saturated fat 3g, Sodium 265mg

1 kg/2 lb	lean leg or neck end of pork, trimmed and cut into small cubes
300 g/10 oz	tomatoes, roughly chopped
1	sweet green pepper, seeded and chopped
1	large onion, sliced
3	garlic cloves, crushed
1 tbsp	safflower oil
1 tsp	cumin seeds
1 tsp	yellow mustard seeds
1 tsp	ground cinnamon
1 tsp	mustard powder
1/2 tsp	ground turmeric
10	black peppercorns, crushed
6	small red chili peppers, fresh or dried
6 tbsp	vinegar
2 tbsp	plain low-fat yoghurt
1/2	lemon, grated rind and juice
1/4 tsp	salt (optional)
4 tbsp	chopped fresh coriander

Heap the pork and all the other ingredients except the salt and fresh coriander in a large non-reactive bowl and mix them together well. Cover the bowl and leave to marinate for 24 hours.

Transfer the mixture to a large saucepan and simmer gently for 1 1/2 hours, stirring occasionally and adding a little water if it appears too dry. At the end of cooking, taste a little of the stew and add the salt if required. Stir in the chopped coriander before serving.

EDITOR'S NOTE: This dish will taste even better if kept in the refrigerator and eaten the following day.

Red Pork

Serves 4
Working time: about 25 minutes
Total time: about 1 hour and 25 minutes
(includes marinating)
Calories 235, Protein 22g, Cholesterol 70mg,
Total fat 15g, Saturated fat 4g, Sodium 180mg

500 g/1 lb *neck end of pork, trimmed of fat and cut into small cubes*
1 *lemon, juice only*
2 tbsp *safflower oil*
1 *onion, very finely chopped*
3 *garlic cloves, crushed*
6 *large red tomatoes, finely chopped*
1 tbsp *tomato paste*
1 tsp *ground turmeric*
8 *black peppercorns, crushed*
1/4 tsp *coriander seeds, crushed*
1/4 tsp *salt*
8 *fresh coriander sprigs, chopped*

Put the pork into a shallow non-reactive dish with the lemon juice and leave to marinate for 1 hour.

Heat the oil in a frying pan and add the onion, garlic, tomatoes and tomato paste. Cook for 3 minutes, then add the turmeric, peppercorns and pork. Cook, uncovered, for a further 3 minutes to brown the pork; to prevent burning, you may need to add about 3 table-spoons of water. Add the coriander seeds and salt, cover the pan and cook over medium heat for a further 15 minutes, until the meat is tender.

Serve in a warmed dish garnished with the chopped fresh coriander.

Beef and Tofu Satay

Serves 12

Working time: about 45 minutes

Total time: about 5 hours (includes marinating)

Calories 145, Protein 7g, Cholesterol 10mg, Total fat 8g,
Saturated fat 2g, Sodium 20mg

3 tbsp	*low-sodium soy sauce or shoyu*
3 tbsp	*fresh lemon juice*
1	*garlic clove, finely chopped*
1 cm/¹/₂ inch	*piece fresh ginger root, peeled and finely chopped*
¹/₂ tsp	*light brown sugar*
¹/₄ tsp	*hot red pepper flakes*
250 g/8 oz	*beef fillet, trimmed of fat and cut into 1 cm (¹/₂ inch)cubes*
250 g/8 oz	*firm tofu, well drained, cut into 1 cm (¹/₂ inch) cubes*
	fresh coriander leaves, for garnish
Peanut sauce	
60 g/2 oz	*shelled peanuts*
2 tbsp	*groundnut oil*
1	*onion, very finely chopped*
1	*garlic clove, crushed*
³/₄ tsp	*chili powder*
³/₄ tsp	*ground coriander*
1 tsp	*light brown sugar*
2 tsp	*fresh lemon juice*
2 tsp	*low-sodium soy sauce or shoyu*
1 tsp	*cornflour*

In a medium-sized bowl, mix the soy sauce, lemon juice, garlic, ginger, sugar and red pepper flakes, stirring until the sugar has dissolved. Add the beef and the tofu and stir to coat them with the marinade. Cover the bowl closely with plastic film and leave it to marinate in the refrigerator for 4 to 6 hours, turning over the meat and tofu occasionally.

To make the peanut sauce, preheat the oven to 180°C (350°F or Mark 4). Spread out the peanuts on a baking sheet and toast them in the oven for 10 minutes. When they are toasted, tip the nuts on to a tea towel and rub them vigorously in the towel to remove their loose brown skins. Put the nuts in a food processor and grind them finely.

Heat the oil in a non-stick frying pan. Add the onion, garlic, ground peanuts, chili powder and coriander, and fry them for 2 minutes, stirring constantly. Add the brown sugar, lemon juice, soy sauce and ¹/₄ litre (8 fl oz) of water, and bring the mixture to the boil, stirring it well. Simmer the sauce until it is the consistency of cream—about 10 minutes—stirring frequently to prevent it from sticking. While it cooks, place the cornflour in a small bowl, add 1 tablespoon of water and stir them together to make a paste. When the sauce is ready, stir in the cornflour paste; this mixture will serve as a binder, and prevent the sauce from separating. Pour the sauce into a serving dish and leave it to cool.

About 30 minutes before you cook the satay, soak 12 bamboo skewers in cold water. This will keep them moist and prevent them from burning under the grill.

Preheat the grill. Remove the skewers from the water and pat them dry on a tea towel. Thread the beef and the tofu cubes alternately on to the skewers and grill them 8 to 10 cm (3¹/₂ to 4 inches) below the heat source, turning the skewers occasionally to brown the meat evenly, for 5 to 8 minutes.

When the meat is cooked, transfer the skewers to a platter or individual serving plates, and garnish them with the coriander leaves. Serve the satay hot, accompanied by the peanut sauce.

EDITOR'S NOTE: The red pepper flakes in the marinade make the beef cubes very spicy. For a milder flavour, rub the meat cubes with paper towels after you remove them from the marinade and before threading them on the skewer.

Cornmeal Pancakes Filled with Chicken Picadillo

PICADILLO IS A HIGHLY SPICED MEXICAN DISH WITH A MINCED MEAT OR POULTRY BASE.

Serves 8

Working and total time: about 1 hour and 15 minutes

Calories 190, Protein 14g, Cholesterol 20mg, Total fat 5g, Saturated fat 2g, Sodium 65mg

75 g/2¹/₂ oz	cornmeal
60 g/2 oz	plain flour
1	egg
30 cl/¹/₂ pint	skimmed milk
2 tsp	corn oil
225 g/7¹/₂ oz	fromage frais
3 tbsp	chopped fresh coriander
1 tsp	safflower oil

Chicken picadillo

500 g/1 lb	ripe tomatoes, skinned and chopped, or 400 g(14 oz) canned tomatoes, chopped, with their juice
1	onion, finely chopped
1	large garlic clove, crushed
1 tbsp	red wine vinegar
1 tbsp	mild chili powder
2 tsp	fresh oregano, or 1 tsp dried oregano
¹/₂ tsp	ground cumin
	freshly ground black pepper
45 g/1¹/₂ oz	raisins
30 g/1 oz	stoned green olives, quartered
	flaked almonds
2 tsp	capers, coarsely chopped (optional)
250 g/8 oz	cooked chicken, diced

To make the pancake batter, combine the cornmeal and flour in a bowl and make a well in the centre.

Break the egg into the well. Using a wire whisk, gradually beat the egg into the flour. As the mixture thickens, whisk in the milk a little at a time. When it is all incorporated, whisk in the corn oil. Cover and set aside in a cool place for 30 minutes.

While the batter rests, prepare the picadillo. Put the tomatoes, onion and garlic in a heavy-bottomed saucepan and stir in the vinegar, chili powder, oregano, cumin and some pepper. Cook the mixture, covered, over low heat until the onion is soft and the sauce is quite thick—about 20 minutes. Stir occasionally, and add a few tablespoons of water if the mixture begins to stick to the pan. Add the raisins, olives, almonds, capers if using, and chicken, and stir everything well. Cover and cook gently until the mixture is heated through—about 10 minutes.

Meanwhile, make the pancakes. Brush a little of the safflower oil over the base of a 15 cm (6 inch) pancake pan, or small frying pan. Heat the oil until it is smoking hot. Stir the batter well, then pour 2 to 3 tablespoons into the centre of the pan and make eight pancakes, stirring the batter well between pancakes to keep the cornmeal from sinking to the bottom. The cornmeal pancakes will be speckled brown on one side.

Lay out the cooked pancakes, speckled side down, on a flat surface. Spoon a little of the picadillo on to a pancake and roll it up; repeat until all the pancakes are filled. Place the pancakes on warmed individual plates and top with the fromage frais. Sprinkle the chopped coriander over the pancakes and serve them hot.

EDITOR'S NOTE: The pancakes can be made ahead of time then filled and reheated in a lightly oiled baking dish, covered with foil, in a 180°C (350°F or Mark 4) oven for 30 minutes.

Duck Brochettes with Spiced Wine Sauce

Serves 4

Working time: about 45 minutes

Total time: about 1 hour and 25 minutes
(includes marinating)

Calories 210, Protein 18g, Cholesterol 70mg, Total fat 7g,
Saturated fat 2g, Sodium 125 mg

350 g/12 oz	*boned duck breasts*
5 tbsp	*red wine*
1/4 tsp	*salt*
1 tsp	*mixed dried herbs, such as oregano, thyme and marjoram*
1/2	*small onion, finely chopped*
125 g/4 oz	*oyster mushrooms, trimmed and wiped*
1/2 tsp	*virgin olive oil*

Red wine sauce

1 tsp	*grated orange rind*
2 tbsp	*fresh orange juice*
60 g/2 oz	*red currant jelly*
12.5 cl/4 fl oz	*red wine*
1/8 tsp	*cayenne pepper*

Carefully remove the skin and fat from the duck breasts. Cut the flesh into neat 2.5 cm (1 inch) cubes.

Put the red wine, salt, herbs and onion in a bowl and mix them well. Add the cubed duck flesh, turning the pieces in the marinade until they are evenly coated. Cover the bowl and allow the duck to marinate at room temperature for at least 1 hour, turning the duck pieces occasionally.

Meanwhile, prepare the sauce. Combine the orange rind and juice, redcurrant jelly, wine and cayenne pepper in a small saucepan. Bring the mixture to the boil, stirring constantly, then lower the heat and simmer the sauce gently until it is reduced by about half. Strain the sauce, return it to the pan, cover and keep warm over low heat while you grill the brochettes.

Preheat the grill to high. Remove the duck pieces from the marinade with a slotted spoon, and thread them alternately with the mushrooms on to small skewers. Place the brochettes on the grill rack and brush them with the oil. Grill the brochettes, turning them once, until the duck pieces are tender yet still slightly pink inside—4 to 5 minutes. Serve the brochettes hot, with the wine sauce on the side.

EDITOR'S NOTE: Other varieties of mushroom, such as chanterelles, ceps or button mushrooms, can be used in place of the oyster mushrooms.